THE SOME PLACE LIKE HOME

Lessons From a Decade Abroad

DINA HONOUR

There's Some Place Like Home

Lessons From a Decade Abroad

Cover design: Claire Waring
Cover image: Pixabay

ISBN: 1729724485
ISBN-13: 978-1729724484

DEDICATION

To Steggs, my dreamer, whose sense of spontaneity and adventure paved the way for this crazy journey. To Rowan and Reed, without whom it would be a lot less interesting. And with far fewer hugs.

CONTENTS

ACKNOWLEDGMENTS

Thank goodness for friend ships which cross in the night. This book never would have happened without endless conversations over coffee, Cava, or a decent Pinot Noir. To those of you I've met along the way, thank you for trusting me with your stories and most of all, with your friendships. From those first dusty days in Cyprus to the endless Danish winters, you have continually made me think, ponder, and appreciate. To my stalwart blog followers and those who share its words, tusind tak. A brief and not nearly exhaustive list: Taryn, Marta, Jill, Caroline, Rup, Erna, Dani, Rikki, JoJo, Jo, Lucy, Julie, Annabel, and Amanda. Thank you to Erin for telling me the truth about my early graphic design forays, to Cherry for the same, and to Kirsten, Louise, Poornima, Meg, Amy, Vanessa, Claire J. for their proofreading magic. And a big thanks to Claire W. for taking charge of the cover design. To my Mother who never doubted, my sister who always encouraged, Lisa, who always cheered from the sidelines, and of course my boys, all three.

And finally, to all the Wicked Women with whom I've laughed and cried, my heartfelt gratitude. You have made it all worthwhile.

FOREWORD

The book world is full of fantastic guides to help navigate the twists and turns of a life abroad. There are volumes brimming with tips; how to thrive in a brand new culture, the best way to master a tricky new language, even meditation exercises to ease the fear your retirement funds will be eaten up by therapy bills for your third-culture kids.

This book is **not** one of those.

In 2012 I started Wine and Cheese (Doodles), a blog about my experiences as a parent and expat, first in Nicosia, Cyprus then later in Copenhagen, Denmark. *There's Some Place Like Home* is a book of stories, lessons, and observations culled from a decade of living abroad. It's not a guide, but a window onto a life lived away from friends, family, and the familiar.

These are the stories of the past ten years. Here are the things I've learned, loved, and laughed about. They are stories of loosing sleep, making sense of the non-sensical, and saying a thousand goodbyes.

What shapes our ideas of home? What makes expat friendships so unique? How does living abroad change you? What kind of mixed-up accent are your kids going to end up speaking with, and where the hell are *they* going to feel at home, especially if you continue to ping-pong around the globe?

For anyone who has ever boarded a plane, train, or automobile setting out on the adventure of expat living, I hope there's a bit of wisdom contained in these pages but even more, I hope you find a bit of yourself—a moment of connection.

I promise whatever you're feeling, you're not alone. You're not imagining it. It is hard...and crazy and adventurous and thrilling and full and sad and exhausting.

There's nothing quite as lonely as stepping foot in a country you've never been to and declaring yourself **home**.

There's nothing quite as exhilarating either.

Somewhere in between is the crazy upside down and sideways life of an expat.

Some place in there is home.

Dina Honour

BUCKET LIST (noun)

The list expats make upon arriving at a new post which contains all the things they want to do while there. Alternatively, the list of 500 undoable things an expat tries to squeeze in as they prepare to leave a posting.

As in: While we're in Denmark, we need to travel to Norway and Lapland and ride a reindeer while watching the Northern Lights from an ice hotel drinking schnapps under a fur blanket.

Wine and Cheese (Definitions)

THE SECOND BEST DECISION I'VE EVER MADE
2018

"It's not always easy being an expat."

How many decisions do you make in the course of your life?

Cereal or toast? (Neither) Coffee or tea? (Coffee) Open the wine or not? (Is it Friday? Then yes!). Life is chock-a-block with decisions, from the mundane to the momentous.

Every now and then you're whistling along happily enough, tearing through the mundane decisions like a boss, when you come face to face with a giant one.

Marry me?

Should we start a family?

Should we buy a house?

Should we open the 2nd bottle? (Is it Saturday? Then yes!)

Sometimes they're expected decisions, decisions you've been quasi-prepping for through your life, but sometimes—just sometimes—they come out of nowhere.

In the back of my brain I knew my husband's job might offer us the opportunity to move overseas. But when you're talking about it, it's all *sure, great, what an adventure, pass the ketchup.* It's in the future. It's the abstract. It's not **real.**

Until he comes home one day and says, "Hey! There's a job opening in Cyprus. What do you think?"

What did I think?

* * * *

Have I told you how much I love NYC? Really? I mean have I *really* told you? Have I told you how the city boogied down deep into my bones until it became part of my DNA? How my sons were marinated in a lullaby of sirens and street noise? Forget *Leaving Las Vegas*, if there

2

was an alcohol-sopped memoir of the mid-section of my life, we could call it Leaving New York.

Leaving the city of my heart, where I fell in love, got married, had my babies was well, it was tough. Like drag me away tough. Kicking and screaming tough. New York, man. It gets into your blood, it seeps into your pores, it worms its way...but enough about New York because I was **leaving it**.

On a jet plane, with two kids, a couple of suitcases, and a plan of action so loose it was jiggling like my post-baby muffin top.

And then there I was, in the middle of the Mediterranean. Me, my two kids, and a yiayia down the street named Poppy. That was it—me and a Greek Cypriot granny. My entire life turned upside down because of one momentous decision we made sitting in bed on a sunny Sunday morning while our second son slept a few feet away in our too-small-for-two-kids apartment.

* * * *

For the first year, I was convinced it was, quite possibly, the worst decision I'd ever been a part of. Worse than the plaid pants with the ribbed yellow turtleneck get-up in third grade. Worse than my Aqua-netted combustible hair in high school. Worse than every shitty financial decision we've ever made. (Note: Should you buy the one-bedroom apartment? Hell, yes you should).

I cried because I missed the election of Barack Obama. I cried watching the ball drop in Times Square on New Year's Eve. My mother and sister came to visit us and when they left, I ugly sobbed on the sidewalk as the car pulled away. It was...not good.

It was in fact, bad.

Really bad.

Of course things improved, even within that first year. As nice as Poppy the yiayia was, I made friends who were slightly closer to my own generation, more Breakfast Club than the Early Bird Special club. But still, it wasn't until after we left Cyprus and, if I'm honest, well into our Copenhagen cycle, that I started to really think about the decision we made all those Sundays ago.

* * * *

It's not always easy being an expat. There are times when it is appallingly hard. Being a family unit without the support of nearby relatives as a buffer can be – well, let's just say intense. Family time, I am often caught saying, is overrated.

Some things about it actually *are* great. Being abroad has given us an opportunity to bond in a way I'm not sure we would've had we'd stayed in New York. This one is born of living a specific experience all together, simultaneously.

Our horizons? Not broadened as much as exploded.

I've learned to stop fearing change, and, dare I say, embrace it. Or at least more so than before. I've gone so far outside my comfort zone, I've gotten jet lag. Bizarrely, I've learned how to relax. Let's just say I'm now type B -- rather than type A.

Living as an outsider in a country that isn't yours, when you don't speak the language, or understand the nuance of the culture itself, often at the mercy of a job, teaches you nothing if not this: you can't control *everything*. Some stuff yes, other stuff, no.

I think, for a long time, I got them mixed up.

It's taught me I really only truly need the people I love around me and a decent wine shop. Should we open the wine? (Is it Sunday? Sure.)

Being an expat has taught me how to offer my friendship...and receive friendship in return. It has redefined my concept of home, on every level imaginable. It has honed my criticism of my own country, but it has also deepened my love of it.

It has given me an understanding of being the odd one out, of being on the back foot, of having to pay attention. It's deepened my appreciation for difference, from the minor to the major.

It's taught me how to bake from scratch and how to live with less choice, and how to use cloth napkins because paper products in Denmark are stupid expensive. Also, that I don't know how I survived as long as I did without an electric kettle.

It's taught me that when someone is meant to be in your life, you find a way to make sure they stay in your life.

This decade-long adventure has allowed us to get to know each other in a completely unfettered way. It's just us over here: no insulation, all family, all the time. No Sunday family dinners, but no Sunday family drama either.

It has, quite honestly, fundamentally changed who I am as a person.

For the better.

So as I meander through the mundane, bus or train? (Bus) Pizza or Thai? (Pizza) Should we open that bottle of wine? (Is it Monday? Then no, you big lush), I can look back at some of the momentous with more clarity.

That decision we made all those Sundays ago, saying yes to taking that chance? It hasn't always been easy, but it was probably the second best decision I've ever made.

The first? He's sleeping next to me.

PRO TIP

Stop Doing Math!

Remember sitting in high school trig class and thinking, *am I ever REALLY going to have to calculate the tangent of an angle?* I am about to make your dreams come true. You can stop doing math. And by math, I mean stop calculating Dollars to Euro to Sterling to Yen in your head. Chances are that wherever you've moved, things are about five times more expensive than you expect them to be. Seven US dollars for a cup of mediocre coffee? You'll get used to it. Or you'll be so desperate after spending an hour in the supermarket looking for peanut butter that you won't blink an eye.

EXPAT VERSION 7.2: SURVIVAL MODE
2016

"...you probably don't realize how much energy you're expending on a daily basis when you're living somewhere other than home."

A friend confided to me, with a mixture of both surprise and exasperation, how much difficulty she's having managing her time. A new job, two youngish kids, a house, a husband, a life, the whites, the darks, the ironing and all the rest.

It's a lot to fit into the confines of the day, I assured her.

"But I didn't have this much trouble back home," she confessed, "and I worked more hours!"

Working less, kids getting older, life getting marginally easier. It stands to reason it would be a cake and Chardonnay walk in the park, right?

Wrong.

To quote my kids in their best nascent whine: "But **why**?"

Here's why: As an expat, you expend slightly more energy than normal. Not necessarily on the big stuff, the stuff you'd expect, but on all the little things you go about in your daily life. Each interaction and action and corresponding reaction requires just a pinch more thought, a dash more understanding, a soupçon more interpretation.

Even though the individual amounts may be small, all that extra effort sucks the life out of your personal battery—just like the programs open and running on your laptop. You know, the ones you don't see or hear but are essential for running the programs you *do* use.

Life outside your home country requires a little bit **more**. You have to run a lot of extras in the background to make sure the **Expat** version you're currently using is the most up to date and compatible with the rest of your life.

And all those extras? They're a drain.

When you're living outside your own end-zone, you exist in a semi-perpetual state of hyper awareness with regard to the small, the every-day. The little differences, the *not-quite-the-same* norms, and the *kind-of different* rules that are innate to the culture you're guesting in. You are more aware of stepping on someone's foot when they don't move out of your way on the sidewalk. (The Danes seem to be constantly engaged in a country-wide game of chicken, both on foot and in cars. And I am perpetually perplexed as to who is expected to yield.)

Concentration is required when you are driving on the wrong side of the road, whether it's the right or not. It takes focus to make yourself understood in another language, especially when you land in the emergency room or if you have a child with a fever. If you're American, there's the added burden of constantly converting temperatures and weight into metric so the rest of the world understands what you're talking about. There is making sense of the strange-sensical. There's often an open app for homesickness and an always-running worry of *what next?* All are things you don't spend too much energy on when you're *inside* your own culture, among your own tribe, when you're 'home'.

Thinking about it all, even unconsciously, takes up a lot of valuable space. It uses too many resources.

Perhaps it's why so many expats look forward to going to whatever Motherland birthed them. Not only to see family and friends and eat gut-busting amounts of their favorite foods, but to let those busted guts hang out; to take a few weeks to shut down and reboot.

Being 'home' allows you to recharge your battery because you only run the basics. There's nothing major lurking in the background sucking your brain dry. Home is usually, *blissfully*, nothing more than Shopping V. 3.4, Eating V. 6.0, and Slothing V. 10.

Just like you often don't realize how much power your computer is actually using until you start getting the black screen of death or the spinning wheel of despair, you probably don't realize how much energy you're expending on a daily basis when you're living somewhere other than home. Is it any wonder then that sometimes the everyday seems a lot more exhausting than you would expect?

So what do you do? Most of us switch out the battery for a new one every few years. You reboot as needed. Sometimes you need to run Disk Warrior in the form of a vacation. Sometimes it helps if you close out a few dead-weight programs you forgot you had running, things like PTA Bake Sale V. 1.4 and Converting Currency V. 4.2. Usually you can free up some space for the latest version of Expat Life V 7.2.8: Survival Mode (tennis, massage and BonBon pack optional).

And it's always a good idea to shut everything down every now and again. I recommend doing it with a glass of wine. And if you need something to read, there's a really great blog I know....

It doesn't matter if you're the one staying or going. You have been a part of something, something bigger than just yourself. Whether it was for six months or five years, whether you played a starring role or a cameo, what you shared was specific to a time and place, to a group of people. It was unique. Sure, for every one missing, someone else will arrive. For every one going, two will stay. But don't be fooled. Numbers don't make up the entire story. It will never be exactly the same because the dynamic has changed.

And that's because of *you*.

NINE EXPATS YOU'LL MEET ABROAD
2014

Millie the Moaner
Millie is never happy. She can't find a cereal her kids will eat. She doesn't like the weather or the people or the way the meat tastes. She moans about the school, the climate, the lack of cleaning products, the local customs, the driving, and the fact that everything is done differently. Millie counts down the days until her assignment is up. She spends her time reminiscing about home with her best friend, Connie the Complainer. You will often find the two of them whiling away the hours in perfect disharmony.

Greta the Go-To Guru
Greta knows everyone and everything. She can tell you where to get your hair done and who to call if your internet connection goes down. She has six different babysitter recommendations at any given time. She's a fixture at school, holding court, doling out dollops of intel. She's the one with a phone full of contacts. If you need advice, you go see Greta. If you don't know who Greta is, just ask. Everyone else does.

Linda the Loner
Like the Yeti, Linda is rarely seen. Her kids take the bus to school and she doesn't engage in playground chatter nor does she attend any events. Sometimes you can put a vague face to the name but mostly she keeps to herself. When she *does* show up to coffee mornings or school conferences you have to ask her name--more than once. Those who mention Linda's name will often be met with a blank stare and a "Who?"

Nancy and Nora the Newbies
Nancy throws herself into anything and everything, stretching herself thin in order to keep herself from worrying that moving abroad was the worst decision ever. Nora can be identified by the permanent smile she

has on her face. Both Nancy and Nora attend all social functions and are often eager and enthusiastic to volunteer. (Side note: this early enthusiasm is usually sucked dry by others. See Millie or Connie above.)

Betty (or Barry) the Bitter Spouse

Betty (or Barry) hasn't quite gotten over the fact that they left behind everything they worked for to follow their spouse around the globe. They are bored, don't know what to do with their time, and that makes them somewhat bitter. Their complaints aren't as focused as Millie's; but spending time with Betty (or Barry) often leaves you with a bitter taste in your mouth.

Sasha the Serial Expat

Sasha often hovers around the edge of the pack, exuding a BTDT vibe. Not quite world-weary, but definitely not as enthusiastic as Nancy and Nora, Sasha has been around the block too many times to get excited. She has had her fair share of run-ins with Millie, has done a stint as a Greta, may have been a Betty at one point and now sees the benefit of Linda's lifestyle.

One-shot Wanda

Wanda and family are on a one-time only expat jaunt. In order to make the most of their time, they eagerly sightsee, travel extensively around the region and throw themselves headfirst into their host country's culture. You will rarely hear Wanda complain, mostly because she is too busy soaking in the surroundings. She's got a bucket list and she's not afraid to use it.

Raquel the Real Housewife

Raquel is the stereotype of the expat housewife personified. Her speech is peppered with words like *massage* and *maid*, *tennis* and *pool boy*. She lunches, exercises and never bemoans the cost of a color and cut. Often her spouse travels extensively and Raquel views her lifestyle as payment in kind.

Tom the Token Dad
Tom is given special dispensation because he's a male. Because of his special status as cock-in-the-henhouse, he is usually either a.) the center of attention b.) tolerated as a pet project or c.) let off the hook because, well, he's a Dad.

So the questions is....which one are you?

EXPEDIT-ION (noun):

The first trip to the local Ikea to purchase the same units you sold before you moved the last time.

As in: *Damn it, I can't believe we gave away the storage cabinets! Now we've got to buy the Expedit units all over again!*

Wine and Cheese (Definitions)

FRIENDS IN ALL THE RIGHT PLACES
2018

"Forget the movers and the shakers, the back room deals and the golf club promises; there is a whole lot of dealing going on in FB messenger chats, closed social media groups and list serves."

Recently a friend announced she was moving to Paris. So I did what any expat would do.

I reached out to a British woman I met in Cyprus who now lives in Warsaw but used to live in Paris to ask her about schools. Then I got in touch with another British woman who lived in Copenhagen before me (she moved to New York and I gave her some tips), and now lives in Paris.

Simple, right?

The British friend from Cyprus who used to be in Paris but is now in Warsaw is soon moving to Ottawa. So I promised her I would hook her up with the folks I know from Copenhagen who are now in Ottawa.

Paris? Check!

Next I got in touch with an American woman and a Kiwi by way of Oz, both of whom I know from Denmark who now live in The Hague to see if I could hook them up with a Brit who came to Denmark via Qatar and is now going Dutch.

Den Haag? Check!

As I was tapping out messages and typing requests, I was astounded by the sheer size and capacity of the global network that hums along behind the scenes. And no one's the wiser.

Forget the movers and the shakers, the back room deals and the golf club promises; there is a whole lot of dealing going on in Facebook messenger chats, closed social media groups and list serves. Got a question about moving your goods from Singapore to Seattle? Post a question and you'll have sixty-four answers within five minutes, from the container companies who will break your Great Aunt Agnes's china to the ones with the hunkiest haulers. Want to know how the schools in Entebe compare with the ones in England? No problem. I guarantee you someone has the answer.

In a lifestyle in which your whole world can turn upside down with one layoff, one big oil company buyout, one dream job offer, information is currency.

And let me tell you, there's a whole lot of trading going on. It's like those old-fashioned telephone operators sitting in front of octopus tentacles wires, connecting one party to another.

Expat Moms. Getting shit done.

Signing the contract is the easy part. It's the rest that haunts your dreams. Having to move is hard. Moving to a country you've never been to before, not knowing where to start? That's paralyzing.

There's a village out there. And it's organized and on social media. It's a whisper network of expats, mostly women, out there helping other (mostly) women. Not for money or fame or fortune, not even for the golden goose of an expat package, but generally just out of kindness, a desire to help, and the kinship which comes with moving to a country not your own.

That ready-made global community at your disposal – it gets lost in all the wheeling and dealing, the packages, the glitz and glamor (as if!) of moving abroad. But it's important.

Information and advice about schools and sports programs, neighborhoods, where to find gluten-free groceries for your celiac child, where the best cardiologist is for your son with a heart problem. How to get around, where to go, what to do, where to stash your mother when she comes for a visit. Buy or lease, take off your shoes or not, what do I need to bring with me from home, how are the OTC drugs?

I have an eight year old, a three year old, and an incontinent terrier. Where's the best place to look for a house and doggy diapers in Dubai?

I need to fly back and forth to care for an ailing parent. Where's the best place in Uruguay to secure an au pair who drives, cooks Thai, and speaks Mandarin?

Don't get me wrong. A package is nice. But so is having a list of schools to look at before you hit the ground, especially if it means you can cross a few off your list. A paycheck is necessary, but on the ground advice about which neighborhoods to skip and which to put on your wish list? That's the real deal.

All of the things which help smooth the transition, which help keep the nibbling anxiety at bay. Schools, housing, childcare, doctors. Tips and tricks. Advice and areas to avoid. Dos and Don'ts. Musts and Mustn'ts.

It's all there. Yours for the taking. Or the asking. You just need friends in the right places.

Or friends who have friends who used to be in the right places who might know someone who might know a gal.

ETA or ESTIMATED TIME OF ACCLIMATION (noun):

The time it takes to fully adjust to a new move, usually one year.

As in: *Don't worry, you won't cry every day after you've been here a year or so!*

Wine and Cheese (Definitions)

LOVE'S LABOUR LOST
(OR WHY YOGA PANTS ARE BAD FOR YOUR MARRIAGE)
2013

"Who knew there was a **best of me**, *like some Greatest Hits album?"*

"Oh," my husband recently sighed. "The *yoga* pants."

Sometimes it takes a cataclysmic event to rock your relationship, to make you sit down and take a good, hard look at your emotional surroundings; a serious illness, an extra-marital affair, a trial or a tribulation that must be faced. Sometimes those head on collisions, those crashes of reality versus expectation, are the tipping point in whether a marriage survives, or whether it bursts into flames on the way down. Summits are called, G8 meetings of marital accord. Contracts are pulled out and scrutinized. They may be renegotiated, they may be declared sound and worthy, they may be declared null and void.

Statistics are on your side, either way.

But sometimes it is not the seismic jolt of matrimonial earth, but a slight shift of a relationship fault line. Something seemingly inconsequential. A subtle shift in attitude, an air of difference, an offhand comment. And sometimes that little something can make you stop dead in your tracks and do an on the ground evaluation. Nothing requiring lawyers and accords and general assemblies, but a spot check if you will.

Like yoga pants.

What's not to love about yoga pants? They are comfortable and marginally more appealing than sweats. They denote wholesome activity. If you wear yoga pants people assume you actually *do* yoga. They may assume you are the type of person who shops at Whole Foods and limits her wine intake and is at peace. They may assume your chakras are aligned after watching the sun rise while in warrior pose. All good

19

things. The problem is, I don't do yoga. And my yoga pants are old. And they're from Old Navy. The only thing differentiating them from sweats is that they don't have a band at the ankle. Otherwise, eh....they're pretty sloppy.

And apparently, as my husband pointed out, they have become the only clothes he sees me in.

Like so many other couples, my husband and I sometimes struggle to find balance. Like many families, we play acrobat and try to juggle the interests of our children, ourselves, and each other. From time to time *our* relationship is the one that gets put on the back burner, thrown onto the slush pile, pushed back in line for take off while we make time for the kids and increasingly, for our own interests. In our case, we have the additional burden of being expats. There is no family around for gratis childcare, babysitting is expensive, and just when you find a friendly teen who gets to know the kids, she ups and move back home. All excuses of course, but excuses which, unless you are careful, push the couple time priority down to the bottom of the to-do list:

Bake birthday cake, wash work shirts, call Mom, fill prescription, call dentist, pack lunches, make gynecologist appointment. Go out to dinner with spouse.

Life is busy. Life is full of other things to do. Life has a habit of getting in the way. It's easy to look at the bigger, overall picture and overlook the details: I love my husband, he loves me. We have a good, solid relationship. Sure, he hates talking about finances and I hate nagging him to call his mother, but overall, it's a solid 8 out of 10. It is easy to rely upon that love and comfort with each other and *isn't it grand that I can hang around in my boxers and stained tee-shirt from college and we still love each other so much* kind of thinking. Until someone calls you out on it. And you find yourself standing at attention for a spot check.

In yoga pants.

"I never get the best of you any more," my husband said. "I get rushing around in the mornings *you* and I get rushing around to cook dinner and put the kids to bed *you*." He looked at me. "And as soon as those yoga pants go on, there's no way I'm getting anywhere near you."

At first I was a little taken aback. Who knew that there was a 'best of me', like some Greatest Hits album I wasn't aware of? But of course we are not talking about my off-key humming and moves like Jagger. We are talking about the me that is not rushing through the kitchen making sandwiches and intervening in the great banana breakfast war, or the me that is not dragging my end of the day self to get the kids into bed so I can sit down and catch up on the news. Or my blog. Or my knitting. We are talking about the me that is struck by a thought I want to write about in the middle of the day or the me that has a stimulating conversation with another parent while chaperoning a field trip; the me that laughs over coffee, or sympathizes over lunch, or enjoys a bit of juicy gossip in the school yard.

The best part of me, when I am actually dressed in real clothes.

How sad it is that the person I *choose* to love—not my children who were a gift or my family into which I was born—but the person I met and fell in love with and choose every day to be with, the one person who should be getting the best of me, *he* is missing out.

Love is being able to be yourself, flaws, warts, grays, chin hairs and all. Sometimes that self is in yoga pants stuffing its face with chips on the sofa watching Downton Abbey on demand. And that's ok. But not all the time. I am not advocating waiting by the door in full makeup with the newspaper and a martini while the casserole burns either, but as a friend said, at least make the effort to wipe away any stray mascara from under your eyes when you hear the key in the door.

Yoga pants aren't really going to ruin your marriage. But the complacency they represent just might. Most of us need to break out the dancing shoes a little more. Even if we're only dancing in the living room after the kids have gone to bed.

On one hand you realize that home really *is* where you lay your head, where your immediate family is safe and accounted for. On another, you realize home is also the place where foundations were laid. *That* home, be it the town you grew up in, the country you identify with, or the longitude and latitude that accounts for the way you tread your way across life's stage, is a place that pulls you like no other. On one hand there is the thrill and excitement of living in a new place, exploring new surroundings. On the other, there is the unshakeable notion that no matter how long you live somewhere, how fluently you speak the language, how adept you become at pretending you like herring in curry sauce, you are never really going to be *home*.

That's a lot of hands. And you still end up with this:

There's a difference between making a *home* and being *home*.

UNDER THE BANNER OF FRIENDS
2016

"You see, in expat life, friend ships that should simply pass in the night but instead go bump is one of the best things about what is sometimes a strange and tiring way of life."

Marta is the first and only Basque I've ever met. Jill is an American Jew. Marta has been our go-to for all things Spanish, Jill when we need to know the right kind of pretzel sticks to make marshmallow dreidels at Hanukkah.

Both are mothers, though the ages and makeup of their families differ greatly. While Jill's oldest was starting middle school, Marta was still changing diapers for the twin toddlers she had at home. Both are married to Americans, both have dogs. And that's where the similarities end. In most circumstances, they'd have been like friend ships passing in the night. In fact, I have trouble imagining a scenario when Jill and Marta *would* have been friends.

But four years ago, they both wound up in Copenhagen.

I may doubt the likelihood of their friend ships meeting in the night, but what I cannot doubt is that over the four years they've shared, they have indeed become friends. *Good* friends. Their husbands and their kids too. They've shared dinners and vacations and parties and inside jokes. For most of that time, I've been a part of that friendship, but I've also had the pleasure of observing it as well.

You see, in expat life, friend ships that should simply pass in the night but instead go bump is one of the best things about what is sometimes a strange and tiring way of life.

It's easy to assume a relationship of differences, one based primarily on the **where and now** would be on shakier ground than one formed on a foundation of similarities and sameness, but often the opposite is true. In my experience, the bond that holds two *different* friends together tends to be even stronger. Maybe it has to be in order to get things to stick in the first place. Or maybe you work harder at it. Or maybe, as I suspect, you look after it a little bit more because you know how unlikely it was to begin with.

Jill and Marta didn't have much in common but they found enough common ground in the cold, Danish soil which welcomed them both. They built on that ground and in doing so, proved sometimes being in the same place at the same time is the only foundation you need.

Of the many friends I've made on this expat journey, most have been unlikely ones. Folks with different political views, different parenting philosophies. Different religions, different ethnicities, different views on life. Sure, I gravitate toward people with whom I have things in common—that's a part of human nature—but the fact that this experience has thrown us together in a giant melting pot—which has then fused together some freaky combos? It's my favorite part of the whole damn thing.

Tazza, my decade younger Aussie friend, mother to only girls, who doesn't swear or like tattoos. Somehow it doesn't matter. Liz, who pulls a different electoral lever than I do. There are Jill and Marta, my age-tribe mates who do swear but differ from me in many other ways. There has been a bevy of Brits, more than you can shake a stick at, most of whom turn a blind eye to my loud, American ways and strange way of holding a knife and fork. Canadian, Spanish, Dutch, French, Norwegian, Irish, Indian. Many of them I have nothing in common with other than being on this gray Danish island together. Together we've scratched our heads over Danish customs and consulted Jeanet, our resident Dane when perplexed. She graciously indulges our curiosity and allows our exasperation.

Yet in the time we've spent together, we've learned to embrace our adopted Danish flag and wave it about. Under this red and white banner which doesn't belong to any of us, but now belongs to all of us, because it is the place we made these unlikely friendships.

This life and these friendships—they've allowed me to shed the weight of *should*. Being an expat has allowed me the freedom to be friends with people I have absolutely nothing in common with other than the flag we're all living under. It's allowed me the chance to explore these unlikely friendships and watch them grow.

It has been one of the biggest and most unexpected gifts I can imagine.

For four years Marta's Basque flag and Jill's Stars and Stripes took a backseat to the red and white Dannebrog, the same way my own colors have taken a backward step to allow me to make friends.

Perhaps it has been the same for you, putting aside differences to gather together under the banner you're temporarily living under–be it Emerati or Swiss or Canadian, Thai or Scottish.

Under the banner of friendship.

PRO TIP

Remember the grass is often greener!

Sure, we miss out on a lot by living away from home. But we get to experience some amazing things as well. When you are uploading the latest trip pictures to Facebook, remember that a lot of people aren't going to remember that you don't get to have Sunday family dinners or have Nana watch the kids for a weekend. Living away from family is always a trade-off, but when your snow-shoveling friends back in Buffalo are seeing pictures of your family frolicking on the sandy beaches of Phuket, sometimes it's hard to see the downside.

IS THIS SEAT TAKEN?
2014

"...in Denmark, I seem to be, at all times, **in the way.***"*

People assume that it's the big issues about living abroad that throw you for a loop: language barriers, cultural differences, whether or not to take your shoes off upon entering someone's house. More often than not though, it's the little things that get under your skin and worry away until they fester and sore and threaten to undermine your life.

In Denmark, for me, it's the general disregard for lining up in an orderly fashion and the corresponding intrusion upon my personal space. What my sister calls 'the bubble'.

I come from the land of plenty. We have things like **big-sky** country, The **Grand** Canyon, grilled meat the size of Texas; McMansions and all you can eat buffets. Big hair, big teeth, big bucks. We like our space, supersized if you please. Here in this land of vikings and Hamlet, however, it seems that I am always in someone's way.

I'm a New Yorker. I have two decades of city walking under my belt. Twenty years of **not** stopping to smell the roses, head-down-I-have-someplace-to-be-don't-bother-me experience. I know which door to use on the train, how to move to the rear, how to exit. I didn't just fall off the majroe** truck.

So it came as a shock that in Denmark, I seem to be, at all times, **in the way**. At first I chalked it up to having no clue where I was. I thought perhaps I just needed to get used to living in another country. Sometimes I had to stop while attempting to sound out a seventeen letter street name. But after nearly a year I now think it's just a different view on personal space...and a general disdain for lining up in an orderly fashion.

This is, admittedly, difficult for me. Even living in New York City, where you were often pressed nose to armpit during the morning rush, there was a sense of space. You know those young men on the subway who sit with legs spread wide enough to birth a calf? They are protecting their space. Sure, there are always folks who ignore the unspoken rules of living in a small space with millions of people, but they are vilified and on the receiving end of many a pre-caffeinated evil eye.

Then there are the English.

I have always admired the English for their public reservedness and apologetic air of being, as well as their joy in queuing, a skill which has been elevated to a national pastime. As the quote goes, *"An Englishman, even if he is alone, forms an orderly queue of one."*

Bliss.

After the laissez-faire, easy-peasy attitude toward rules and order in Cyprus, I had high expectations for Denmark. And while the Danes are great at forms and signaling in the bike lane, I continue, much to my dismay, to have people **UP MY ASS**.

I admit to indulging in more than my fair share of treats since our arrival (did you ever wonder where Danishes actually *come* from?), and to having put on a few extra pounds. Still....with two kids and a husband, even *with* the extra padding, there is no room up there for anyone else. On the street, in the bike lane, on the train, in the line for immigration, in the supermarket, in a box with a fox or in the rain with a Dane—whichever way I turn, there is someone right there, **thisclose.**

Every culture has its quirks. Every culture has things which seem normal within the map lines of their own country but come across as bizarre or puzzling to those who weren't raised there. The Danes are no different. There's a funny piece called *How to Piss off a Dane* someone sent me when we first arrived in Copenhagen. Rather ironically, it waxed poetic about how much Danes value privacy in the public sphere. In my experience, this protection of privacy doesn't translate into not feeling up the person in front of you, it just means they don't actually *acknowledge your existence* while they do. The entry which really stuck with me however, which made me chuckle, was the insistence that a

Dane would, to paraphrase, *climb inside your backside if only to be a few inches closer to the front of the line.*

I laughed. I thought it was a stereotypical exaggeration. A bit of funny hyperbole.

I was wrong.

No matter where I turn, there's a Dane. **Thisclose.**

****majroe** is the Danish word for turnip. I thought I was being clever, but it occurred to me no one's going to know what the hell I'm talking about.

EMOTIONAL JET LAG (noun):

What you feel upon returning home from a trip *home*, when your heart is in two places at once.

As in: *I can't wait to get home but I know I'm going to miss home as well.*

Wine and Cheese (Definitions)

REAL HOUSEWIVES OF COPENHAGEN
2013

"As an expat housewife, I live in a bubble. It's cushiony and large and full of things my bubble back home wouldn't have room for. But it's a false reality."

When we first made the decision to move abroad I was regaled with stories of **the Help;** maids and house cleaners and au pairs and chefs and personal umbrella holders. No dishpan hands, no fighting with the vacuum, free time up the wazoo. Laundry sorted and folded and put away with afternoons free to tra-la-la through local museums and fiddle-dee dee through quaint cafes.

Ha.

Snort.

Guffaw.

Oh, without a doubt, the *don't lift a finger* scenario is true in places. Parts of Asia are well-known on the expat circuit for having stupidly inexpensive household help. The further east you go, the further your dollar goes. And honestly, how many of us would turn down a little extra help with those stubborn stains and tub rings if it cost pennies instead of pounds? Sometimes geographical or political instability, language barriers or safety issues make hiring help a necessity rather than a luxury. A good friend and her family accepted a posting in a *Stan,* an entity that didn't feature on quizzes when I was cramming for world geography in Mr. Kowalzyck's 8th grade class. Because of political turmoil and the nature of her husband's job, they are shadowed by bodyguards and are required to have a driver.

Not so for us.

When we took off from the US, we landed squarely in the Euro Zone. We left behind not only family and friends but cheap consumer goods, affordable take-out and utility bills that didn't go beyond three figures.

On one hand we were grateful to accept a posting in a relatively secure country–at least one in which the leadership had not been accused of boiling its political enemies alive–but on the flip side, we also landed in a place that made New York seem cheap. Hell, it even made London look cheap.

As an American, I am spoiled. You cannot get a true idea of how cheap consumer goods, electricity and yes, even gasoline are until you spend time outside of the US. Cyprus was expensive. Copenhagen is extortionate. Not just touristy/airport/five dollars for a slice of pizza pricey, but well and truly expensive. There are reasons the Danes are consistently voted the happiest people on Earth; one of those reasons is that the minimum wage comes in at about twenty USD an hour.

If someone paid me twenty dollars an hour I wouldn't mind the scrubbing and the food shopping so much.

Nevertheless, I clean my own house. I mind my own kids. I shop for the best prices with my pocket translator in hand and a conversion rate in my head. I have dishpan hands and mounds of laundry and am constantly lacking some necessary dinner ingredient.

In short, I do what most housewives do, only I do it in a different country.

So what do the real housewives of Copenhagen, or Tashkent, or Bangkok or Hong Kong or Panama City do?

We run the gamut. Some work while they are abroad, trying to find balance, juggling family and career. (Sometimes you get lucky and land in a place like Denmark which places importance on work/life balance). Some lunch and play tennis. Some volunteer at school or head the PTA or join a local networking group. Some get to follow their dream of penning a novel.

We seek out comfort in what can sometimes be uncomfortable situations, looking for the familiar in the unfamiliar. We do our best to make a home in a place that's not home. We kiss skinned knees and get frustrated when the person in front of us in the express line has more than ten items. We fight with our spouses about finances, we count down the days to vacation. Our lives sometimes seem exotic, but more often than not, that is no more than a by-product of where we end up. My kids have seen the pyramids because it was an hour flight from Cyprus. They have never been to Disney World, it's always been too far away.

Those expat wives who spend their days lounging and lunching and being massaged and coming home to cooked meals and folded laundry and children who are already in bed? Chances are they would be doing that no matter where they were. That is a certain lifestyle, the kind that usually comes with enough money that whether you are stretching your dollars in Shanghai or shortening them in Stockholm, it's not going to matter too much.

As an expat housewife, I live in a bubble. It's a lovely bubble, don't get me wrong. It's cushiony and large and full of things my bubble back home wouldn't have room for. But it's a false reality. It's like being on vacation but doing your job while you're there. I'm not out getting massages, I'm trying to figure out which cut of meat translates to one I can cook in twenty minutes. I have free time during the day, but I lack the village to back me up. It's a hop, skip and a jump to a European vacation, but it's a twelve hour journey home. There are perks, but no Granny's shepherd's pie or Nonna's babysitting service. There are great friendships, which are too often cut short by moves.

Real expat housewives? We worry about our kids, fret about our finances, navigate the supermarket, burn the toast, sort the lights from the darks, fight with our husbands.

And if you are me, spend a great deal of time scrubbing stubborn stains and trying to get the ring off the tub, all whilst dreaming of the sales in New York and cheap take-out options.

EXPAT SPEAK

Q: How are you finding it here?

Translation: Are we going to be friends or are you going to be the person I strategically avoid for the rest of the school year? This is not to be confused with genuine concerns. For instance, if someone says "It's harder than I thought it would be," seasoned liver-abroaders generally go all mother expat hen and spill their best tips about navigating the supermarket. But if the answer is "Ugh, the (fill in your guest country's folk here) are so rude"? Pretty much going to keep the social interactions to a nod and not much more. There are whole pockets of naysayer expats. They will find a place amongst their own tribe and be happy in their own unhappy way.

GUILT TRIP
2016

"A one-way guilt trip is bad enough. But expat guilt is a roundtrip. Not only do I feel guilty about what the adults are missing, I feel guilty about what the kids may be missing too."

There are certain things you take with you from post to post. The linens and the towels, the housewares and the bedding. Favorite books and photographs and items that remind you of home(s). Sometimes when you move across oceans or over latitude lines on the globe it can be a good opportunity to chuck out the ratty old stuff you've been hanging on to, to embrace the symbolism and start fresh. Sometimes though, the ratty, old things are the ties that bind and so into the packing boxes they go.

One of the heaviest things, one of the biggest space wasters, yet one of the hardest to let go of, is the guilt that follows you from map dart to map dart.

Expat families may take more trips than their more rooted contemporaries. But the guilt trip is never one we look forward to.

It's possible I feel that heavy weight of guilt more keenly due to mitigating circumstances: Italian, raised Catholic, mother. The Holy Trinity of guilt. Seen from an outsider's perspective, it's easy enough to justify picking up your immediate family and moving thousands of miles away. After all, it's your life to live, it's your future to grab by the ovaries. Those opportunities out there, the ones ripe for the picking? They are yours for the plucking.

Seen from the inside, through the filter of the guilt trifecta, it can be difficult to justify the very same thing: picking up your immediate family and moving thousands of miles away.

There are families who don't have a real choice, those who knew the fine print when they signed on the dotted line. But for many of us moving abroad involves an active decision. There is a choice, an opt-out, a chance to say 'no'. For my family, the reasons *why* were as wide and varied as the straphangers on a Downtown 6 train. But at the end of the day, it was a choice. And that choice, though ultimately and sometimes heartbreakingly the right one for us, meant our families would be deprived, by virtue of time zones and geographical space, of their children and more importantly, grandchildren.

Unlike the middle-aged spread which is harder to shift and gets in the way of your pants buttons, the moving away guilt is not there all the time. Most of the time you're so caught up in the day-to-day business of life you probably don't stop to think about it too much.

And then something stops in your tracks. A funny story you want to share only the time difference is too great and someone is deep in a REM cycle. A sporting win or close loss. A girlfriend. An award, a violin concert, a story to share. An American penny where an American penny should not be lurking. Sometimes it's nefarious and sneaky and catches you off guard. Sometimes it hits you in the gut like a sucker punch.

Guilt.

I am grateful for my life, but that doesn't mean I feel guiltless when it comes to the way we've chosen to live it. I feel bad that my mother only sees her only grandkids in six month intervals. I feel bad that she doesn't know what clothing size they wear just by looking at them or what their interests are. I feel bad she doesn't get to watch them blow out birthday candles. I feel bad my in-laws don't get to see them open presents or cheer them on from muddy sidelines or listen to their goofy jokes. I feel bad my sister and sister-in-law don't get to have holidays all together without maximum planning and redeeming frequent flyer miles.

I feel guilt that this life we've chosen was the selfish choice. Not always. But sometimes.

A one-way guilt trip is bad enough. But expat guilt is a roundtrip. Not only do I feel guilty about what the adults are missing, I feel guilty about what my kids may be missing too.

Is it fair to inflict this nomadic lifestyle upon children? Are we giving them a gift or setting them up for heartbreak? Are we teaching them skills they'll need to compete in a global world or are we screwing with their ability to make lasting, lifelong connections? My children have gone from apartment to house to apartment again. They've never experienced the joy of a backyard swimming pool or a neighborhood to grow up in, of friends they've seen every day since kindergarten. They won't have any of the same kind of memories of growing up that I have, or that my husband has.

Lifestyles have changed so much in the time between then and now, it's likely they wouldn't have anyway. But that doesn't stop guilt from speeding down the road and picking me up for a little joyride every now and then.

When are you coming back? When are you coming home? When do you think you'll settle? Where do you think that'll be?

They're not meant to be more than voiced curiosity or a genuine desire to know. But sometimes in the wake of those questions comes a whole bag full of guilt. Bushels of it. Boxes and barrels of it. And let me tell you, when the movers come around to do a survey to see what's going to fit in your next shipment and what isn't?

That guilt takes up a helluva lot of room.

AMAZING RACE, THE (noun):

The act of trying to squeeze in everything you want to do before you leave a posting.

As in: *We've been here for three years and still haven't ridden on the reindeer sled or woken up in an ice hotel.*
See also: Bucket List

Wine and Cheese (Definitions)

CAN DAD COME OUT TO PLAY?
2013

"In this topsy-turvy life, he doesn't have the same opportunities to seek out new friends, or to nurture those friendships."

Once upon a time, in a place far away, my husband and I had a lot of friends. Our dual income/no kids New York life was exactly what you imagine a dual income/no kids New York life would be. Late nights out, lots of work, lots of disposable income. Brunches and Sunday crosswords and giant martinis sipped on the roofs of hotels. We were spoiled by take out choices, twenty-four hour bodegas, and a transit system like no other. And then, in the space of a busy nine months, we switched to a one income/one kid family and every aspect of our lives changed. Our social life took a nosedive. Eventually the gravitational pull of finding friends with kids won out over trying to coordinate schedules with those friends without, and though we did our best to maintain those **Before Children** friendships, I will be the first to admit they suffered.

When I was lucky enough to find a mom I got along with, it was like winning a bingo game. As the kids got older, started walking and talking and pushing and biting, if my children liked the children of my friends, it was like hitting the jackpot on a slot machine. When a friend and I finally went all in and attempted **the family outing** and the men got along? Forget it. It was like hitting the jackpot, the lottery and bingo all at once.

We were lucky, we hit the lottery a few times in New York.

And then we moved.

Amazingly, after a three and a half year stint in Cyprus, our social life had never been so good. Cheap childcare, a car, a good group of friends, inexpensive meze and we were out more than ever. No martinis on roof tops, but that's undoubtedly a good thing when you have a six am wake-up call in the form of a warm, squirming child. We were getting comfortable, starting to talk about vacationing with other families.

And then we moved.

There are a lot of things about a life abroad which are harder on the non-working spouse–especially when it comes to closing up shop in one country and opening it in another. You know, the boring spreadsheet stuff: closing out accounts and turning off the gas, freaking out over the lease terms and trying to figure out how to turn on the electricity when you can't even speak enough of the language to "press one for English". But there's one thing I think is often more difficult for the working partner: making friends.

I'm an open book, (I talk a lot), and I have a pretty easy time making friends, (I talk a lot). In addition, I have school-age kids.

School, both in Cyprus and in Denmark, is where I've met the vast majority of my friends. My husband doesn't have a day-to-day presence at school. He's got....work. And while he enjoys the people he works with, after spending eight hours a day, five days a week with your colleagues, sometimes the last thing you want to do grab a beer with Hal from accounting or June from the front office on a Saturday night. Understandable.

The problem is, now he has no friends.

That's not true of course. He has very good friends. There are the 'boys', five or six who grew up together, terrorized their small suburb together, grew into men together. They were each other's best men at weddings, are god-fathers for each other's children. But as adults, they are scattered all over the globe, and short of weddings, all of them being in the same country together at the same time is a rare occurrence. He's got friends back in New York, he's got friends in Cyprus. He has a lot of friends. It's just none of them live in the same country. And so, after a year in Denmark, I find myself asking other women, "Does your husband play golf? Does he watch football? Drink beer?"

I'm not pimping him out. I'm making playdates for him.

I'm not alone in this. Most of the women I've met on the expat circuit do the same thing. It's a little like a Dad dating service, except you don't need to worry about flowers or STDs. Family time is great, in small doses, but we all need to blow off steam, to bitch and vent about our spouses and families to a willing ear. And it is always nice to do something we find enjoyable. Bonus points if it's something your spouse hates doing.

Our kids are old enough that I don't need to make sure the little one isn't shoveling Lego bricks into his mouth or the older one isn't putting a fork into the toaster. We don't need to worry about nap schedules or diaper bags or the stroller wheels fitting through the shop door. But for a long time, my husband's interests got put on hold so that he could help out at home. Playing football with the lads gave way to being home for dinner, helping with baths, and if nothing else, adding an additional voice of reason in the otherwise insane witching hours that constitute dinner, bath and bedtime. He curbed the weekend golf, but he wasn't sitting around singing *The Itsy-Bitsy Spider* in music class and homing in on the one other mom who was rolling her eyes. The afternoon pint or three down the pub was forgotten, but he wasn't spending hours bonding with others who were exasperated by Cypriot driving skills.

By not doing that, he was missing out on the biggest chance to meet other people like him, with similar interests or concerns.

In this topsy-turvy life, he doesn't have the same opportunities I do to seek out new friends, or to nurture those friendships.

The man may beat me at Scrabble every time we play. He may make better scrambled eggs. But I've found something I'm better at: making friends in strange, new lands.

So for now I'll make a few more Dad dates.

Golf, anyone?

PRO TIP

Wear nice socks!

When in doubt, take 'em off. Shoes, that it. Use other people's behavior as a guideline. If there's a big old pile of shoes by the door, don't saunter into the classroom in your new Marc Jacob heels, no matter how fabulous they are or what a great deal you got on them. Depending on where you are, it can range from slightly rude and messy to downright blasphemous to keep your shoes on. So make sure your socks match your outfit, your tights don't have holes in them or pack a pair of bunny slippers. When in doubt, ask your host. It is better to be seen as slightly ignorant of a local custom than to mortally offend your host, not to mention mark up those reclaimed wood floors with your heels.

THE LONG GOODBYE
2016

"I've spent the better part of eight years saying goodbye. And it really doesn't get any easier."

For the better part of the last eight years my life has been a constant stream of goodbyes.

I said good-bye to my beloved New York City. I said goodbye to Cindy, to Carol, to Britt. To Grand Street and McCarren Park, to the L train and to twenty years of the Big Apple. I said goodbye to working, to take-out, to MetroCards and friends who had spanned two decades, more names than I can list here.

I said good-bye to my family. To my mother. To my sister. To my Nana. I said goodbye to driving on the right side of the road. And by right, I really do mean right.

I said goodbye to everything I knew, everything that made my life comfortable, everything that was routine, from food shopping to dialing the phone to simply walking out of my front door.

And in nearly eight years, I haven't stopped saying goodbye.

Four months after landing in Cyprus I said goodbye to Sally, my first Greta the Guru. The crazy mom whose name I can't even remember disappeared off the face of the Earth in there somewhere too. Then it was Liesl, whose house we spent so many hours at, who gave me the greatest description of irrational rage ever, who my youngest son called Mama Liesl for a long time. Then Sara, then Donna, Cindy, Kirsten. Goodbye to Clare and Simon.

And then we had to say goodbye ourselves. To Dorien, Angie, Victoria, Tim and Miriam, Janna, Serene, and Sophie. To Katie and Paul. To Judy-Mou and Nikki. To Krisztina. To Eliza and Paul and Birgitt and Fiona. To the school my son learned to read at. To the nursery where my younger son learned how to make friends. To the play groups, to the heat, to the dust and tumbleweeds. To the beaches, the baba ganoush, to the atrocious parking and driving on the left. To that dusty island itself.

Of course there were untold numbers of goodbyes in between. Goodbyes to family who came to visit, to summer vacations when we relaxed and let our breath out only to have to suck it back in again upon our return. To my Aunt Kathy who died not long after we moved abroad, to whom I never got to say goodbye. We said goodbye to lost teeth and baby-hood, to diapers and strollers. I said goodbye to the very idea of having another baby (though my husband said goodbye to that one a long time before).

This crazy life we lead. It seems as soon as we say hello, we're saying goodbye. There hardly seems a breath between. In Denmark I said hello and goodbye to Dana, our paths crossing only long enough for an invitation to coffee and a ride for my son to his very first school disco. A goodbye to Jill who I felt like I knew, even though I didn't.

Then to Kara, gone on the fly the day after school started. To Beth and Tim, to Inge, to Nici. To another lovely Clare. Then to Sara–midwestern foul-mouthed knitting gal. That was a year of thick and fast goodbyes, when it seemed everyone left at once, leaving a heart-shaped hole behind. I said goodbye to honorary-American but thoroughly British Lucy. To Helena and Sally, Jennifer and Kim and Martine. Goodbye to Renee, to Ann, Karin and Lisa too. To Ainsley who tried to sneak out without telling. Claire, Melissa and Barbara. Goodbye to Louise, here only a year. Goodbye to Natalie and Theo. To Pippa, whom I was only just starting to get to know. I said goodbye to Stefan and goodbye to Carrie, and to the lovely Leontien not long after. There were so many that year we started a new tradition at school just so we could all say goodbye. And we waved our flags and hugged our hugs and we cried our cries.

Because goodbyes, for all you practice them, suck.

And I wonder: Are there other lifestyles so bursting with goodbyes as the one we lead? This life, with the looming reality of eventual goodbye tattooed onto your every encounter, woven into the lifestyle, tied up in the very nature of it all.

It makes my heart ache every time I watch a group of teary-eyed children say goodbye to a friend, to a classmate, to a teacher. It doesn't hurt any less when it is a group of adults. We have our traditions, our rituals, our goodbye dance. Here in Denmark there are flags and circles of appreciation for the children. Signed tee shirts that will sit unworn in drawers. For the grown-ups there are coffees and teas. Parties, presents, and promises. There are hugs. More tears.

I said goodbye to Lindsey, Jo, and Nelly. To Elizabeth and Patti and Zuzanna, Marnie and smiling Susan too. I said goodbye to Dani and Jay, the nicest Canadians you'll ever meet. I said goodbye to Andrea, to Polly and to Nicole and her boys.

A difficult goodbye to my walking partner, Sunday dinner friend Tazza (and my de-facto god-daughter, Emma).

And now before I can catch my breath, another goodbye to our songbird Jo, to be forever known in our family as JBNS. A few more flips on the calendar and I will say goodbye to Jill, to Liz, to Andrea and Maridith. To Avril, to Anja and Sandra, Rikki and yet another lovely Claire. To our resident celebrity dad, Claudio. Eventually to Cristina from the block. There are more, but you know that I know that others don't know, so suffice it to say your names are here in spirit until contract t's are crossed and package i's are dotted.

Eventually we will say have to say goodbye to Denmark ourselves. When we talk to our kids about the eventuality, there is sadness. One night my older son said, in the type of stilted, choked-up voice that makes you doubt your capacity as a parent, "I don't want to have to say goodbye to my friends."

Before I could even say I understood, before I could read him the love letter of people, places and things that I carry around in my heart, he wiped his eyes and said: "But I guess if we had never come here, I never would have met them at all."

I've spent the better part of eight years saying goodbye. And it really doesn't get any easier. But my son is absolutely right.

The lump in the throat and the sting in your eye, the quiver of your lip as you wait your turn to say goodbye, yet again. It's all worth it.

Because just think, if I hadn't said that very first goodbye, I never would have had all of this.

DOG YEARS (adjective):

A way of describing the quick intensity of expat friendships which seem to compress time.

As in: *We've only been friends for a few months, but that's like a decade in expat years.*

Wine and Cheese (Definitions)

THE EDAMAME PROBLEM
2014

*"It's a champagne problem, of course, this act of fitting into a
lifestyle you weren't expecting."*

A few months back, I was chatting with a friend, a fellow expat
who is moving home.. She and her family are relocating from a fairly
swank zip code here in Denmark (Copenhagen 90210) to a rural village
in the north of Scotland. Narrow, windy roads and fertile fields. Small
Beatrix Potter-esque woodland animals popping out from behind the
hedgerows sort of stuff. She is excited, but a little worried about how her
son will deal with settling back into what repatriating expats might call
'real life'. While their new village lifestyle might be more along the lines
of how she grew up, her son has grown up very differently.

The only real school her son knows is the private, international
school my own boys attend. She's worried that he'll be lagging behind in
a few subjects, sure. She's concerned he'll have to adjust to a more
traditional, test-based system. But the real core of her worries is that
he'll have trouble fitting in with kids who've gone to the local school with
each other for the whole of their lives. That he'll stand out as different.

That he will, to paraphrase her concerns, get the shit kicked out
of him for being soft.

"The other day he asked if he could have edamame for a snack!"
She told me, slightly aghast.

In that one sentence, in that flummoxed, perplexed, 'how on
earth did a child that I raised grow up asking for edamame as a snack?'
look on her face, she summed up everything that many of us worry about
when we enter into the often cushy bubble of expat life. Because let's
face it: many of us wouldn't be living the lives we live now if we were
back home. Many of us *won't* be living the lives we live now if and when
we repatriate. And unless you had some sort of Asian connection
growing up, most of us probably didn't even know what edamame *was*

until we were adults.

I've been thinking about 'the edamame problem' since my friend and I spoke. Then it came up again, in relation to an article about 'elite volunteerism' at schools, which prompted a lively conversation on another friend's Facebook page and the 'edamame issue' came up again.

I grew up in a blue-collar, working class house in Massachusetts. The most exotic we got in the way of food was the *Ah-So* sauce my mother used to smother the pork chops in every now and again. My first experiences with 'ethnic' food were not until long after I moved away from home. My friend's son wants edamame for snack. My own son has, on more than one occasion, asked for sushi for lunch. These are kids who go out for sushi the same way we had take-out pizza when I was growing up. Sure, it's healthier and yes, it's great that they're exposed to a variety of foods from across cultures, and admittedly it's kind of cute to brag (just a little) about how much your toddler likes a good tuna roll...

So what's the problem?

As the article hinted at, there's something just a little elitist about sushi. And if I'm being honest, expat life for my family is a little like sushi. Or edamame. Sure, it's healthy to expose ourselves and yes, it's great that we are living in another culture and admittedly it's kind of cute to brag (just a little) about the fantastic opportunities my children have....

The edamame problem.

My own family is living a life that, while not exactly false, is not exactly *real* either. Had we been back in NYC, our boys would likely be going to a zoned NYC public school. There would certainly be some kids eating sushi and edamame, but there would likely be many more who qualify for free hot lunch. Regardless of the income bracket fluctuations, there probably aren't middle school ski trips to Germany or "away" sports matches in The Netherlands at P.S. 321.

Like my friend, I feel I often walk the fine line between gratefulness that my children get to experience this privilege (let's call it what it is) and horror that their upbringing is so far removed from my own and that of my husband. There are times we have been left scratching our heads wondering how the hell we ended up here, immersed in this (admittedly lovely) lifestyle that is not very...*us*. My children are able to have this amazing experience of living abroad, but it's not exactly like they're immersed in the society we live in. Sure, the required language lessons give them just enough Danish to order a Danish and they ride their bikes everywhere, but they're not exactly marinating in the special seasoning of Danish culture that churns out more Danes. Essentially, they're privileged kids who are leading a privileged life due to the fact that their father was offered a position overseas.

And metaphorically, nothing screams privilege more than edamame and sushi.

So when my friend was fretting about how her son's new classmates would react if he bandied about words like edamame, I understood exactly where she was coming from. Maybe your kids like sushi. Maybe they like to sit down and listen to *This American Life* with a bowl of steamed edamame. But while it might be de rigueur in the expat world, outside of it, there's a fairly narrow demographic band that is going to say "Oh, my kid too!" If you know you're going back to a place where it's more Ah-So than sashimi, these thoughts can keep you up at night.

It's a champagne problem, of course, this act of fitting into a lifestyle you weren't expecting. This life, beyond anything I could have imagined, is as foreign to me as the land I'm living in. There are some who approach this life of privilege from a more familiar place. Perhaps they grew up with edamame too. Others, like me, find this alternate reality of Friday night sushi slightly jarring.

When I was growing up, if someone had a heated pool, it was a good sign they were rich. There was one family in my neighborhood who not only had a heated pool, but above the mantelpiece in their living room, there was an oil portrait of the family matriarch. At ten, I thought it was the classiest thing ever. A sign of true wealth. Who else but the

50

very rich would have an oil portrait hanging over their fireplace?

Sometimes now, walking through this life that feels as if it doesn't really belong to me, I feel the same way I did when I was ten. Looking at the things around me and thinking: who else but the truly privileged would have these things? Things like sushi for lunch.

Things like edamame.

EXPAT SPEAK

Q: How long have you been here?

Translation: Are we going to like it here or have we made the mother of all screw ups? When someone asks how long you've been somewhere and the answer is a.) more than six months and b.) they have a smile on their face, it's a good sign. When your answer, like mine, is *nearly six years*, you can almost hear them exhale. Generally people don't stay around in a posting for more than a year or two if they hate it. Note: If they're on a fixed schedule, a la Embassy families, you'll get that answer in this question too: "Two years, we've got one more year before our time is up". Embassy families have expiration dates. Like milk.

A TRAILING SPOUSE BY ANY OTHER NAME
2015

"We are so much more that. We are the ballast on the other side of the scale."

Trailing spouse.

It's a term most expats are familiar with and many, including myself, use for lack of a better alternative. A fellow expat's musings made me re-explore my feelings about the term. Truth be told? The more I think about it, the less I like it.

If I was on the fence before, her vivid description of *toilet paper stuck to the bottom of a shoe* made me come down firmly on the side of dislike. Because in a nutshell, trailing spouse has the implication of someone following behind and picking up all the debris and crud the person in front of dropped along the way.

The last person in a race trails. Burning exhaust fumes trail. A caboose trails. Spouses shouldn't trail. Who wants to be compared to a caboose toot tootling along behind the shiny diesel engine?

More than insinuation or semantics, what bothers me most about the term is that it doesn't take into consideration what the non-working partner of an expat actually *does*.

As a trailing spouse, it means from 9-5 my husband is able to focus solely on his job and his career. As a trailing spouse, it means school is never going to call him in the middle of a meeting and ask him to come and pick up the one kid who has nits or the other who just puked all over the teacher. As a trailing spouse I am there to soften the blow of an international move. As a trailing spouse, I learn the lay of the land, get things set up and keep all the day-to-day stuff oiled and running.

For the working spouse, think about what this means in terms of productivity, in terms of career placement and advancement, in terms of availability. As a trailing spouse it means when my husband needs to work late, he can do so without worrying there's no one home when the kids need help with their homework. As a trailing spouse when my husband is told he needs to go away on business, he doesn't have to clear it with the school schedule or vaccination appointments and birthday party obligations. He packs his carry-on and off he goes.

I'm not implying that working expats have it easy, not at all; but working expats who have a non-working spouse, the one typically referred to as trailing, have a cushion which allows them the freedom to focus.

Being a trailing spouse sounds an awful lot like being a stay-at-home-parent and it's true, the family with a stay at home parent reaps many of the same benefits. But there is one huge difference when you're doing it as an expat.

As a trailing spouse, when my husband's job says jump, I call the shipping company, pack the boxes, and we jump. Having a non-working spouse as an expat means you are free to advance to Go, collect your $200 and set up shop in the next location. It means if they want you on Mayfair, you move to Mayfair. If they want you on Boardwalk, you take a chance and roll the dice and off you go. Not having to factor in a second career so you can move around the world in eighty days is a big thing.

Before we left the US seven years ago, I was working, but I wasn't heavily invested in a *career*. If I had been, chances are we would never have accepted the offer to move. By doing so, I sealed my fate for a few years, BUT....I also shored up the foundation on which my spouse was building *his* career.

Being a trailing spouse does not mean I am a nothing but a cheerleader for my husband's job. It doesn't mean I'm selling myself short or prostrating myself to further his career aspirations. It doesn't mean I've shackled myself to his job to keep myself in some sort of lady of the manor way. I'm not picking up after him, following him around and making sure he has clean underwear on in case he has an accident. For now my being home as a trailing spouse allows him the freedom to advance his career, a move which benefits not only him, but our family as a whole.

We are a partnership. I'm not a tag-a-long. I'm not an afterthought.

Far from trailing, I'd argue I'm more of a foundation spouse. A vertebrae spouse. I firm up the family with a solid baseline. I make sure the whole structure isn't going to come crashing down on us all at any given moment. I do all the systems checks and the maintenance to make sure it's not just a house of cards, but a home.

I'm not a caboose.

I'm a spouse. I'm a partner.

Even the term accompanying spouse still denotes tagging along for the ride, not pulling your own weight.

We are so much more that. We are the ballast on the other side of the scale.

So, until we can think of a better term which accurately encompasses all that a non-working expat spouse allows and does, how about we just say **spouse**?

Deal?

MULTIPLE PERSONALITY DISORDER (noun):

The act of being able to navigate between your expat life and your regular life, putting one personality on hold; or the act of adapting to your new surroundings with a wholesale change of routine/wardrobe etc.

As in: *Driving on the wrong side of the road, pretending you like pickled herring or keeping mum about the highs and lows of expat life when you're visiting home*

Wine and Cheese (Definitions)

CULTURE CLUB
2014

"Where do you come from? On the expat circuit, the standard answer is 'How long have you got?'"

The boys' school held their annual Cultures Day festivities the other day. Cultures Day, in case you're wondering, is a day for the school to come together as a global community, to feast on culinary creations from Perth to Poughkeepsie, and to celebrate the melting pot of diversity that is the International School.

In theory.

In reality, Cultures Day is a day to lament the lack of a cool national costume (India *always* wins), to stress over whether you can get the mac n cheese there while it's still warm (score one for American cuisine) and trying to recall the colors of the Estonian flag for the inevitable moment a third grader asks you to paint it on her face (it's blue, black and white, for what it's worth).

But long after the pizza and the schnitzel, when the aebleskiver has finally stopped repeating and you're left scrubbing cheese sauce that has set like cement on your casserole dish, you are often left with the inevitable aftertaste of life abroad. You know what I'm talking about: the unanswerable questions you can taste on your tongue. The bitter uncertainty, the sweet second guessing, the back of your mind worry that taking your children out of the familiar, away from their people, is going to screw them up well and truly.

My ten year-old asked me once if I had a best friend growing up. Sure, I answered him, her name was Kristen. Where was she from, my son wanted to know. Err.....I said, she was from down the street. Yes, he persisted, but where did she *come from?* He couldn't wrap his head around the idea that I had a friend of the same nationality who grew up in the same town, the same state, the same country that I did. Cultures Day would have been a breeze for Kristen or me. One flag, one anthem, some sort of super-sized, preservative laden, color-doesn't-exist-in-nature culinary creation (see: mac n cheese above). Done and dusted.

It isn't always so easy or straightforward for expat kids. Last year I did flag face painting and had kids coming to me with a laundry list of nationalities.

"Well, my mom is Cuban and my dad is German and I was born in Qatar but I lived in Scotland before we came to Denmark.... so can I have five flags?"

Never mind the fact that I had to bring my son's atlas with me for reference, that there were kids asking for flags belonging to nations that didn't exist when I was in school, there was simply not enough time to grant the muddled nationalistic face painting preferences of all these kids. I would have still been there, looking up the Croatian flag (red, white and blue with a checkerboard crest).

It begs the question, however. What was an easy question for me, for my husband, for Kristen and the vast majority of folks I know is a perplexing one for my own sons and their schoolmates.

Where do you come from?

On the expat circuit, the standard answer is "How long have you got?"

The question of identity is a big one. There is a sense of comfort and belonging that comes with cultural identification. Not only the colors of a flag or a fondness for a certain spicy dish of course, but the very notion of a people, *a tribe*: a group with identifiable and recognizable expectations and traditions. Your tribe is who you turn to for answers, for support, for understanding. For backup. When I try to explain the simple beauty of a peanut butter and Fluff sandwich to non-US parents, they look at me in confusion... and a little bit of disgust. And to be fair, I feel the same about Marmite. There is a lot more at stake than sandwich spread preference of course. How much of our sense of self, our identity, comes from where you *come from* vs. where you *live* – because for almost every kid attending an international school, those two things are different.

Many of these kids have parents that hail from two different countries and are growing up in another. Attending an international school should be a way for them to feel at ease, at home in any or all of those cultures. But does it work? To an extent. Though my sons' school hosts students from more than seventy nations, the biggest, loudest contingent is from the US, with the UK running a close second. Watching the primary school's parade of flags the other day, I was reminded of the opening ceremony of the Olympic Games: a sole athlete representing Burkina Faso and, later, a 400 strong Team USA. Just because the numbers are bigger and the voices are louder doesn't mean American culture is more important than that of Burkina Faso, but I would be lying to you and myself if I pretended that a lot of rich cultural traditions don't get swallowed up in the American machine, even abroad.

Because my own kids are (half) American it works in my favor. I imagine if you hail from one of the 68 other nations that are under-represented, it poses a bigger challenge. Not only are you living in a culture outside of your own, away from your tribe, but the international community that forms your new tribe must seem awfully westernized.

What does that mean for the kids from India or the ones from Gabon or the ones from Ukraine? Will they retain enough of their home culture to feel that they have a people, a tribe? Where will their sense of identity and community come from? Will the expectations they are taught at home or in smaller pockets within the international community at large be enough to form a sense of self?

Which sandwich spread will they gravitate toward?

Perhaps in the end these expat kids, growing up in this bizarre soup of nations, will eventually form their own global culture made up of a little bit of this and a little bit of that. A true melting pot of tradition and expectation. Perhaps they will feel equally at home within two tribes, or even three.

Questions to ponder when you are digging out the lederhosen and paging through the atlas trying to find out what the flag for Moldova looks like (blue, yellow, red with an eagle holding a shield) next Cultures

Day. Perhaps by then, I'll have soaked off enough of the cheese sauce to use my casserole pan again.

It is difficult to explain the feeling of bidding farewell to people you've cried with and laughed with, people who know you better than you could have imagined, all the while knowing there is a good chance you will never see them again. I understand why it may seem easier to sneak out, avoid a scene, avoid the tears.

Don't.

Say goodbye. It's important. For a sense of closure, to tie it with a bow, to leave it finished.

I know folks who don't want to make a big deal of their departures for a myriad of reasons. They don't like to be the center of attention, they haven't wrapped their own thoughts around leaving, they don't want to make a fuss or put anyone out of their way. They would rather slip away: unnoticed, un-feted, un-celebrated. They want to walk away without a goodbye.

Don't. That's cheating.

NINE EXPATS YOU'LL MEET IN A GALAXY FAR, FAR AWAY
2016

Yoda the All-Knowledgeable.
The grande dame, Dowager Countess of your international galaxy. Yoda has been around so long no one remembers when she got there; she's just *always been* there, sitting in a corner. Sometimes she talks in cryptic Yoda-talk, referencing a time long gone populated with strange names you don't recognize - i.e., before your time. But she's the one who's got all the dirt on expats past, present, and possibly future.

Han Solo the Too-Cool-For-School Rebel.
Han's been around the galaxy a few times. No stranger to long-haul moves, Han's used to moving at warp speed on short notice, or in the dead of night. A bit cock-sure, a bit swag-a-licious, Han comes across as a little aloof but the teflon attitude is usually just a by-product of a life hopping from one place to the next. Han doesn't get too close to others because, at the end of the day, leaving folks behind is tougher than you think.

Darth Vader the Evil Head of HR.
You know Darth, the one who wants you to move to Burundi. Tomorrow, in the middle of your kid's senior year of high school. The one who needs your spouse on the ground in East Timor next week, which is Christmas. The one who seems to be lacking any humanity in regard to moving small children, pets, and teenagers across borders and seas. Soulless, bleak, and an easy villain to hate.

R2D2 the Fun Expat From the Country You Can Never Remember the Name of.

You introduce them as Russian when they're really Ukrainian; or Czech when they are really Slovakian. Azerbaijan? Kyrgyzstan or Kazakhstan? Tajikistan or was it Turkmenistan? Often their name is a confusing strings of letters you are not used to seeing together and so, in your head, you develop a coded nickname. It's not lack of caring as much as the fact R2 holds a passport from a country that didn't exist when you were studying World Geography.

Obi-Wan the Do-Gooder.

Obi-Wan is the expat who travels to places most of us have never heard of or have no desire to visit, all in the name of good. Usually attached to an NGO or other international organization, Obi-Wan packs up and heads her family to the deepest jungles and barren plains of places you vaguely hear about on the news – usually related to pandemic outbreaks and civil wars. A slight aura of virtue hangs above Obi-Wan's head but most of us happily allow it – because we're glad it is her and not us.

Princess Leia the Spoiled Expat.

Chef, gardener, maid? Check. Check. Check. Leia has usually done at least one stint in Southeast Asia where household help is part of the contract. Sometimes Leia finds herself at a bit of a loss when she's posted someplace where the gardener doesn't come with the lease. She also looks pretty damn good in a gold, lamé bikini. This is usually due to devoting her days to looking her best.

C3PO the Know-It-All.

Whether C3 has been in six countries or one, this opinionated expat will insist there's one *right* way to do things, from moving to assimilating, what to eat or dealing with local custom. Armed with books and articles and surveys and lists, C has processed all of this information and filtered it down to black and white, right and wrong. C is just waiting for someone to slip up to offer an "I told you so". There's little room for nuance in C's bubble but, if you can stomach the sometimes righteous attitude, there's a whole lot of info in there too.

Rey the Rookie.
Rey vacillates between bug-eyed amazement and practiced nonchalance. Her first time out, Rey is desperate to experience everything but doesn't want to seem too eager. She's heard the stories, and only half-believes what life as an expat is like. But just because she's young and green don't sell her short. Dismiss the new girl and it's likely you're missing out on something special.

Boba Fett the Mercenary.
Boba is the expat who takes postings based primarily on the money. Ruthlessly planning their global journey based on the exponential growth of their stock and retirement portfolio, the Fett family bounces from post to post chasing the cash. Hardship duty stations, war-zones, the far-flung corners of the globe. There aren't many places Boba won't go if the price is right.

May the force be with you as you try to figure out just exactly where you fit in.

PRO TIP

Don't get hung up on Please and Thank You!

Cultural norms vary. It can be difficult getting used to the fact that you may have moved to a place where someone cheerfully lets the door slam in your face or elbows their way into a queue without a backward glance. I know, I know–it doesn't take much to give a nod of appreciation when you let someone out into traffic, a quick two finger raise off the wheel, a smile, a "fine, and you?". But in a lot of places, it's *just not done*. No harm is meant, but I can tell you first hand it's infuriating. I promise no one is intentionally setting out to make your life miserable, it's just different. But barring a situation that would put you in contempt of courtesy, don't let it stop *you* from minding *your* manners. Keep on with your pleases and your thank yous. You won't be here/there forever, right?

THE GRASS IS ALWAYS GREENER ON THE OTHER SIDE OF THE OLIVE GROVE
2013

"Looking back, it is impossible to tease out whether it was Cyprus or life itself that was making me miserable."

We landed in Cyprus in late October. Though the blistering heat of summer had mellowed somewhat, there was plenty of evidence of those scorching months in the parched landscape which greeted us; a dead and withered view that stretched from the airport into the capital. Beige and olive drab and lifeless.

Honestly, it could have been Tatooine.

Things did not improve in the next few weeks. A playground stumbled across looked like something out of a communist era moonscape. Rusty seesaws rested upon buckled and cracked asphalt, uneven and dangerous. A neglected aviary housed featherless and sore-infested birds who could have been Patient X for avian flu. Privately, we referred to it as The Park of Death. The American in me feared the entire country was a giant lawsuit waiting to happen.

Determined, we explored a local monastery and found ourselves meandering through groves of orange and olive trees in tin soldier formation. My sinuses started to twitch. My eyes started to water. My nose began to run and sniffle and snort. It became apparent to me that my allergies and olive trees were not going to get along. My husband, fighting to accentuate the positive, stopped and plucked an olive from an overhanging branch.

"Look!" he said, popping an olive into his mouth.

Which he promptly spit upon that dry and cracked ground, because as everyone knows, you don't eat olives raw.

That little olive spitting vignette became my go-to metaphor for our early years in Cyprus. A not yet brined anecdote which captured the whole experience of picking up and moving to a foreign land. For giving up the comfort of the familiar for the adventure of the unfamiliar, saying good-bye to family and friends and jobs and homes and affordable consumer goods and essentially going it alone.

Be it Nicosia, Copenhagen, Bangkok, Pretoria, London, Houston, Dubai or indeed Tatooine, no one tells you what to do when you don't like the place you've landed.

Cyprus is a hot, dusty, insane in the way that only prolonged exposure to extreme heat can make you, kind of place. There is Mediterranean impatience and passion, wild gesticulating and arguing and an ingrained love of confrontation. There is a lot of steam blowing which incorporates screaming and hair pulling and arm waving and getting out of cars to bang on the hood of the car in front. This is, inevitably followed by a swift invitation for a frappe and souvla. If you aren't used to it, it's a huge culture shock. I was coming from New York, where people were crazy, but in an affected, purposeful way. I was miserable.

Looking back, it is impossible to tease out whether it was Cyprus or life itself that was making me miserable. I had an infant who didn't sleep. I had gone from working in New York City, the kind of "bring-your-kids-into-the-office" part-time, freelance gig that mothers dream of, to being a housewife. I was a two plane ride minimum from home, stranded on a hot, dusty little island in the ass end of nowhere. Even now after nearly two years in Denmark it's difficult to separate my feelings about Cyprus from other changes that were happening–each change in and of itself enough to make you pull your hair out and invite someone over for souvla.

Many people tell you they would kill for the opportunity to live abroad. Most of them are thinking of the travel and the full-time help. But depending where you land, those stories of full-time cleaners and personal chefs and days spent lounging by the pool never materialize. When we moved from Brooklyn to Nicosia, I became a housewife. And here in Copenhagen, I remain, a housewife. I do all the things everyone else does, only in an unfamiliar place with unfamiliar products that cost six times what I think they should (remind me to tell you about the time I put the drain cleaner in the kettle by mistake). In books and movies and stories, most only see the adventure part of being an expat. The exotic opportunities. The perks. But the reality of expat life is never what it seems on paper. The problem is, who do you turn to if you're unhappy? How much of a tool do you sound like if you complain? *Yes, I'm living on an island in the middle of the Mediterranean. The average winter temperature is just under 60 degrees F. There are incredible travel opportunities at our fingertips. Our kids get to go to private school. We get to live in a house. And I'm unhappy.*

Even I wouldn't like myself (and I didn't).

You can go the misery loves company route and hang out with the moaners, there are always those that complain mercilessly about the weather, about the food, about the people, about the driving, about the cost of living, about everything else; but by doing that you risk alienating the people who can point out all the good things. And, barring moisture farming on Tatooine, there are almost always good things. You risk getting caught up in a circle of negativity that does nothing to help alleviate the feelings of unease or doubt or unhappiness.

Expat life can be lonely. It can be isolating. It can be incestuous and mind bogglingly petty. It can be clique-y and if you find yourself on the wrong side of the school sandbox, it can be devastating. Chances are when you are a serial expat, you are mostly associating with other expats. Depending on where you are, the international community can range from gated and insular to varied and diverse (in an educated, middle class homogenous kind of way). But up and down that circuit, you are likely to come across the same people again and again.

There may be guilt and resentment, especially if you blame your working partner. It can be difficult not to fall into the "if it weren't for you and your job we wouldn't be in this stupid country and I would be enjoying a bagel in New York" cycle. It took me three years to realize how devastating my initial unhappiness was to my husband. Not only was

I actively unhappy that first year, the things we were hoping to happen career wise for him weren't happening. And we were, essentially, stuck. I don't do well with stuck. I need an out, a Plan B. And Plans C and D. I need to know the emergency exit can be manually opened if and when we needed to sound the alarm. My husband bore this tremendous burden. He was dealing with his own lunatics on a daily basis, he had a wife who was unhappy, an infant who didn't like to sleep, pinworms (another story), plastic melting temperatures and he was trying his best to figure out how to fix everything without breaking the *only in emergency* glass.

Thank God for wine.

You have to soak and marinate for a while in order to absorb some flavor. Bitterness needs to be mellowed over time. It takes a few months of stewing and soaking to let the richness burst onto your palate. In the end, time is what worked for me. I learned to appreciate the mild winters and the cheap babysitting. I learned to drive on the wrong side of the road. I stopped blaming my husband for a joint decision that we had taken very seriously. We made some amazing friends, traveled to some amazing places and had some incredible experiences that we never would have had if we hadn't landed on that dusty rock in the middle of the Med. Oh, and my son started sleeping through the night, which never hurts.

At times, to my surprise, I even miss it. Especially the souvla.

STOCKPILING (verb):

The act of stocking up on essentials when you return home, ranging from shoes to beauty products and over-the-counter medications to Goya black beans.

As in: *Did you pay the airline for the extra bag?*

Wine and Cheese (Definitions)

SHOULD I STAY OR SHOULD I GO?
2015

"Sometimes when you're an expat, especially one who has been stationary for a few years, life starts to resemble a Clash song."

Last week I had lunch with some friends. We moaned about Copenhagen prices, discussed the pros and cons of a liquid lunch and made plans to do drinks soon so that we could get more in the er...*spirit* of things without having to worry about picking up the kids from school. Inevitably the conversation turned, as it almost always does among a group of expats, to that old chestnut of a question:

"So.....how much longer are you going to be here?"

Sometimes when you've been stationary for a few years, life starts to resemble a Clash song. And while *London Calling* surely fits someone's future plans, in many cases, it's more *Should I Stay or Should I Go?*

There are certain postings which have an expiration date built in. Before you put your tray tables away and your seat in an upright position you know when you'll be leaving. There are other expats who are beholden to the whims of the economy, to tax issues or visa limitations. Some get pushed out by nothing more exciting than good old-fashioned cost of living. Some worry about aging family members back home or the right time to move the kids. Whatever the reasons, many of us find ourselves caught in what I call **Expat Limbo**.

Expat Limbo is that special place just above hell when you're forced to start seriously contemplating the next few years. Expat Limbo is when you *could* stay, but then again... you *could* go. You could move on, move home. You could take another posting. Or you could just stay put. The result is often a never-ending loop of *what ifs*.

What if we left now, took the first job that came up that gets us home...or what if we stay?

What if we stay another year and then move home...or what if we stay another year and go somewhere else?

What if we take another assignment for two years and then go home...or what if we take another assignment and the kids are the wrong age to move schools?

What if we take another assignment for two years, squeeze one more two-year jaunt in there after that, and then go home...or what if we just stay here?

What if we just bury our heads in the sand because it's too complicated to figure out?

It's enough to make your head spin. You get all Excel about the whole thing, making lists, creating spreadsheets that factor in the considerations: job security, pensions, leaving behind what has become familiar, saying goodbye to friends, the thought of leaving behind a life you've invested in to start somewhere fresh, *even if that somewhere is home*.

For many of us, school is a massive factor. There are exams to sit to insure places even if you don't know where you're going to be or when. There is the agonizing 'is it going to be easier to move your kid at the beginning of a 'big' year, say the start of middle school or high school, or does it not make a whit of difference' question. There are private vs. public, IB vs. Non-IB, international vs. local issues to contend with. There's the time of year, school years and cut offs dates that change depending on what hemisphere you're going to. And that's taking *one* child into account and assuming there are no special challenges to consider.

The truth is, there's no easy way to do it unless your kids are young enough not to have started school, old enough to have finished, or you are on the list for Hogwarts.

When you're in Expat Limbo you can't make any concrete plans until the contract is signed. What seems like a sure thing often has more holes than a sieve. At the same time, you need to be prepared, so you do your due diligence, rate your research, start making inquiries. You get excited...then a deal falls through. You have a prospect you know would be a brilliant career move but well....Bulgaria? You never really fancied Bulgaria, though you've heard it's lovely in the spring. Maybe you're not so secretly happy when it doesn't happen even if it would have meant a promotion and the acquisition of a household staff.

Adding a little salt to the by-now festering wound of indecision? Most of the time you can't even talk openly about it. The one time you really need to spit it all out and see if it makes more sense than it does in the jumble sale of your head and it's all hush hush/keep a secret. Current employers don't know, you're locked into a confidentiality agreement, your spouse has threatened you with divorce sans alimony if you breathe a word to anyone. And yet someone is always asking:

"So....how much longer are you going to be here?"

You play your hand close to your chest. I've met some people who were so good at holding an ace up their sleeve that I didn't even know they were leaving until they didn't show up for school the following term. Ninja expats, stealthily slipping from one post to the next.

Expat life has heavenly perks and hellish downsides. Yet it's that middle ground, the Expat Limbo, that purgatory of *what ifs*, which can be the hardest time you spend abroad. What you really want more than anything, even more than your favorite food products from home, is for someone to come along and answer the question for you.

Should I stay or should I go?

When you're in a foreign country alone with your children, finding a village to anchor yourself to isn't a luxury, it's a necessity.

You need someone who's going to pick up your kids from school if you're down for the count with the flu. Or someone who you can call in case of emergency. You need sustenance and daily nurturing. You need a tribe. You need a village. You need a community, a group who can shoulder some of the burden of doing it on your own in a place where you likely don't even speak the language or get confused by the currency.

When you find that tribe? Hang on for dear life.

THE TERRIBLE, NO GOOD, VERY BAD DAYS
2015

"At certain times my Facebook feed looks like I go to parties night after night. Glitter and sequins and dress up. Champagne and toasts and friends and ha ha ha, la di da."

Last week I put together a slideshow for a good friend who is leaving Copenhagen. I watched it with my husband, smiling and getting a little teary. As the music faded and the presentation ended with a slick little slide reading *The End*, he looked at me and said:

"Wow, anyone would think we had loads of friends and an amazing life."

Putting aside for the moment that we **do** live an amazing life, he's right.

Most of us don't document the shittier aspects of our day-to-day lives. I don't whip out my handy little point and click to take pictures when I'm playing Old Mother Hubbard and my cupboards are bare and so the poor husband got none. I don't fill my Twitter feed with pictures of myself in sweatpants and leg warmers. (Yes, I wear leg warmers and you will never convince me they are not awesome. Take your leg-warmer hatred elsewhere, haters.)

The pictures we post may not be photoshopped but they are the glossy, edited versions of our life. At certain times my Facebook feed looks like I go to parties night after night. Glitter and sequins and dress up. Champagne and toasts and friends and ha ha ha, la di da. It's probably even more evident if you're an expat. Albums of parties and vacations, it must seem that day after day is nothing but fun and frolic and friends.

There is a subtext to those pictures of course. Those parties? Lots of them are to say goodbye to dear friends. Those holiday meals? They're in lieu of the ones we can't spend with family. Exotic vacations? They're often cheaper than a flight to Florida from the east coast of the

US or the cost of a week at Center Parks. Most of us don't add that stuff in to our posts.

Just as I don't generally share photos of myself in the supermarket going up and down the aisles looking for peanut butter because it's not where I would expect it to be. Or trying to figure out exactly what that cut of pork is on sale (fyi, pork neck is gross, even when it is on sale). I don't post pictures of what I look like after dropping the kids off at school in the Danish rain. Don't be fooled. The rain does not fall mainly on the plains of Spain. It falls incessantly in Denmark.

We all want to present a glossed up, souped-up version of ourselves. Filtered and angled and cropped so we look our best.

But the truth is life is not like Instagram. You can post inspirational quotes until the organic, grass-fed cows come home. You can pledge your allegiance to the flag, to yoga, to cross-fit or to antidepressants. Life it still not going to be like an Instagram feed. Even a sardonic, satirical, sarcastic version of it.

We all have days like Alexander from the famous story book: terrible, horrible, no-good, very bad days.

I'm having one today.

In two weeks a very dear friend is leaving Copenhagen. Christmas is coming and the goose isn't getting fat, but...let's just say my jeans are tight. The bank account is getting the opposite of fat. Danish winter, despite the cheerleading exportation of hygge, *sucks ass*. It's gray and wet and miserable and really DARK. The entire floor of one room is covered in Lego. I've been neglecting my kids, my husband and my friends in order to finish the final draft of my novel, only to realize I'm not really done. Not even close. Last night, staring at yet another round of edits, I gave up. Maybe I'm just not cut out to write a book.

Yup. I'm having a horrible, terrible, no-good, very-bad feeling mighty sorry for myself kind of day.

No one wants to hear about the day-to-day crap. Doing the school run on bikes in the rain, or doubting yourself or realizing you're shouting at the people you love because you're frustrated. No one wants to see or hear how long it takes you to get through to the electrician because you can't understand the language telling you which button to press or the frustration of feeling like you're doing something wrong whenever you step out of the door because you don't know the rules. No one wants to see pictures of the ratty sweats and the leg warmers or the puddles or the un-plucked eyebrows and unbrushed teeth. So we show them the dolled up versions. Not only of ourselves, but of our lives.

So, just in case you think I lead a life of glamour, I assure you I don't.

I am blessed. I am lucky. I work hard at the things that are important to me.

Sometimes, despite all that, I feel sorry for myself.

I just don't generally post about it. But maybe I should, because we all have no good, terrible, very bad days.

Even when living abroad.

CULTURAL ADAPTING (verb):

The act of finding adapters for all your electrical appliances from various countries with various plug shapes and voltage requirements.

As in: *Why can't there be a universal voltage initiative?*

Wine and Cheese (Definitions)

FOUR AND A PIZZA PIE
2016

"And sometimes that's all you need, just a little, tiny bit of normal and right to hang on to."

Not too long ago my husband and I sat down to confront the eventuality of leaving Denmark. Though we have no firm plans, if I've learned anything in the last eight years, it's that mental preparation is half the battle. At some point the eventualities turn into possibilities and the possibilities morph into certainties, usually the day after you book a long-haul flight or fork over half a year's tuition. But in the throes of hashing out the pros and cons of staying vs. going, conversing about how hard it will be to set up camp somewhere else and say goodbye to a damn good life, a life which gets harder to leave every additional year we stay, we boiled it down to this:

As long as the four of us are together and there's decent pizza, we'll make it work.

Because at the end of the day, what more do you really need?

It's not easy. Several good friends have been struggling with repatriation or new country postings. Several more are already anxious at how they'll handle moving home themselves. But as they make the list of pros and cons, of fears and anxieties, I say the same.

As long as you have your family and a deep-dish, it will be ok.

You'll be ok. You'll make it work. It may take a while. It will probably take a while. In fact, I'd be surprised if it didn't–it *should* take a while. Settling into a new place or resettling into an old place, which can be just as foreign and intimidating as a new one, isn't easy. There will probably be a lot of tears. Some resentment. An argument or twenty. A lot of second-guessing. That old bugger hindsight will come into sharp focus.

But have faith that as long as you're together, you'll figure out how to make it work.

You've slogged this road before. You've thought it out. You've run the numbers, listed the pros, calculated the cons. You've looked at it from every different angle and sideways. You'll be ok.

Maybe you underestimated how different it would be, or how difficult. Maybe it's not going to be the best country you ever lived in or the nicest house. Maybe you'll need to hire a tutor for you kids to catch up or maybe your kids will be ahead and lose some of their momentum in the place you're going. Maybe you won't have the same friends you had before you left to go away. Maybe you're going to miss the place and people you left behind.

You'll be ok.

Because as long as you're together and you can get a decent slice of pepperoni, it means there's something normal and right in the world. And sometimes that's all you need, just a little, tiny bit of normal and right to hang on to.

Maybe this move isn't going to be the one that pays off the mortgage or sends your career into the stratosphere. Maybe the commute is going to suck. Maybe the school will suck or the weather or the driving or the lack of decent black beans. But you'll be ok. Because, pizza.

You'll make it work. You'll find a school. Maybe it won't be a perfect fit. Maybe your kids will be behind or be ahead. But it's ok, because they're there with you. You'll find a house. Maybe the bedrooms will be too small or your landlord will be a dick. But the roof will cover all of you. You'll make friends. They may not be as good as the ones you made in the last place, but that just means you made some great ones that will always be there. You'll be able to drive from your house to Ikea and back again without consulting the GPS. And rest assured, Ikea has the same stuff *wherever* you land.

It might not be pretty and neat, but you'll figure it out. You'll figure out what the important things are, like the thickness of the pie crust and the sauce to cheese ratio.

To those of you leaving, those of you who recently left, you'll be fine, I promise. Maybe not today, maybe not tomorrow or even next week or next month, but you will: because you've already got 95% of what you need to make it work right there with you.

You just need to find the pizza place.

PRO TIP

If you can't say anything nice, don't say anything at all!

We all have our complaints. The weather, cultural differences, having people up your ass all the time, the language complexity. But although we call this place home for a while, we are, essentially, guests. And most of us on an expat package, let's face it, have a pretty easy time of it. Sure, the beef doesn't taste the same as it does back home. You can't import Marmite because it is fortified, a stamp costs $2.40 and a tank of gas sets you back about $100. But when you're tempted to stop and complain, stop and think. You are living, and living well, in someone else's country. Their home. Take your shoes off, accept the expensive coffee, and if you don't have anything nice to say, don't say anything at all.

THERE'S SOME PLACE LIKE HOME
2018

"I've left behind horcruxes, filled with pieces of us in
all the places we've been."

When it comes right down to it, I'm just a small town girl.

Home in that small town was a blue, three-bedroom ranch and my yellow-walled room at the end of the hall, a photograph of shiny ballet shoes and a set of gilt-edged encyclopedias on the shelves. Home was the woods with low rock walls and the short cut through to my backyard. Long before Frozen's Elsa, there was the Newman's Elsa, the hound from hell, who strained at her chains as we belted along the fence line. It was pools like skipping stones in green backyards and the cracked pavement which led to the bridge. Home was the womanly curves of the neighborhood itself.

Just a small town girl who took the midnight train going anywhere. Well, a bus to Port Authority at any rate.

Then home was Brooklyn and the East Village and Upper Manhattan and even Chinatown for a month. It was midtown then the LES, then Brooklyn again, neatly closing the circle. It was the F train and the L train and the Uptown 4/5/6. It was city sidewalks and tiny tenements and metal fire escapes which wrapped around buildings like urban ivy. It was pizza by the slice and bodegas and Marlboro Reds and the Indian restaurants along 6th Street with their winking Christmas lights. It was walk-ups and siren wails and bus fumes and energy that bubbled up inside your veins before it burst free through the subway grates in song.

Home was seven hundred square feet of prime hipster real estate in Williamsburg. It was Grand Street Playground and McCarren Park and concrete turtles which dribbled water in endless August heat. It was the crazy woman downstairs, then someone else, then the college kids who hated my toddler--even when I left them birthday cake and beer.

Assholes. It was the sun setting over the East River, Joe's Busy Corner, and Rachel and Tommy who sat on sagging lawn chairs in the sweltering Brooklyn summer. It was the feast of Mt. Carmel and its carnival barkers outside our bedroom window.

For twenty years I made my home in New York. In 2008 I left the city of my heart, packed my memories in tissue paper and carried them across the ocean. I packed up our physical home and watched as it was shoved and crammed into boxes and bound in bubble wrap and rolls of clear, plastic tape. I filled out insurance forms and prayed the ship wouldn't sink.

On the other end we waited. We unwrapped and unwound and unpacked.

All to try to make a home.

The physical stuff, the furniture and the linens, the pots and pans and water glasses, that's easy enough. A pillow. A blanket. A place to lay your head. A fork, a spoon, a coffee mug.

Home in Cyprus was the pink house at Egnatias 5 with its unforgiving tile and the air conditioner that rained hail pellets onto my bedroom floor. It was the coldest house in the hottest place I've ever lived. Home was our local praying mantis and the bitter orange tree, the parade of stray cats prancing through the dirt. Home was a backyard figs and hot pink oleander leaves which fell like colorful rain. It was dusty parks and stunning beaches, crazy drivers and frothy frappes.

And then the movers came again.

Home in downtown Copenhagen was bike lanes like the autobahn and wiennabrød and eight dollar bagels. It was walking to Tivoli and the 2A bus and narrow sidewalks and designer playgrounds. It was public transport and my pink, Danish bicycle. Now home is marginally more suburban; an apartment with ten foot ceilings molded so beautifully you want to cry. Home is the high street with fourteen ice cream shops, it's park life and beach life and city life all rolled into one.

The physical home is easy. I've created homes wherever I've been.

A pillow. A blanket. A place to lay your head. A fork, a spoon, a coffee mug.

It's the other stuff that's tricky.

When your roots don't go deep into the soil of the land where you live, home becomes something else. It's a memory, a friendship, a marriage, a child, a step in a career. It becomes less about the cups and the plates and the pillows and the linens and more about moments strung together like jewels we wear around our necks.

In the summer, home is the one I grew up in, with forty years of secrets hiding in the basement, tucked away in cardboard boxes damp from mildew. From time to time home is the house at the end of the cul-de-sac where my husband grew up, its ghosts, after twenty-one years, nearly as familiar as my own.

Home is where we go to dear friends in NYC who put up our ever-growing sons and their ever-growing appetites. Or other friends who've put us up for a night or a week in the places they call home. Home is the bigger number of those friends who always offer to.

After ten years I have one foot in and one foot out, neither here nor there, and yet both. I've left behind horcruxes, filled with pieces of us in all the places we've been. They're buried, like a time capsule of who I was, of who we were, in that particular time and place.

Home is a stone I carry with me, worn smooth and polished by the pad of my thumb.

Dorothy may have clicked her heels and declared there's no place like home, but she was not 100% right.

There's some place like home wherever I look.

EXPAT SPEAK

Q: Where do you come from?

Translation: How am I going to have to adjust my own personal language/speech/topic patterns in this conversation? Alternatively it can mean "help me out because I can't place your accent". I have trouble with South African vs. New Zealand. Unless they say "shame" in which case, it's South Africa for the win every time. But unless I directly ask someone to replay the Cersei/nun showdown on Game of Thrones, that one can be a bit tricky.

Bonus: If the answer to this question is "The US" or "The UK" it will be followed by a question designed to determine who you voted for or how you voted on Brexit. Whether or not you mentally walk away from that person when you figure out the answer is up to you.

THE CIRCLE OF EXPAT LIFE
2014

"Some of us transverse the circuit once, others go around so many times it's dizzying."

If the 3,485 viewings of the movie *Cars* taught me anything, it is that while life may indeed be a highway, getting from point A to point B is rarely straightforward. There are on- ramps and exits, turn-offs and shortcuts. Sometimes you find yourself out of gas in a small town in the middle of nowhere. Despite my own neurotic push for things to be linear and collated, tidy and neat, most of the time the path we take resembles more of an arc than a line. Sometimes you realize that you've followed the curve all the way around and you are right back at the beginning. Full circle.

Life abroad is no different. We go around in a circle; of adjustment, acceptance, settling in, disillusionment and withdrawal. Some of us transverse the circuit once, others go around so many times it's dizzying. Though everyone experiences life outside their culture differently, there are some standout phases of the circle of expat life I think most of us will recognize.

Phase One: Panic on the Streets of London

The movers have been, the plane tickets purchased. The stuff you're not taking is in storage, goodbyes have been said. Often that's when the real panic sets in: the questions you can't answer, the ones that keep you up at night. Will the kids be okay, will they make friends or is this going to screw them up even more than they are already screwed up? Will *you* make friends, will the school playground be full of cliques? Will you learn the unspoken rules of a new culture? What if you forget when and where to take your shoes off ? Will you be able to find your favorite cleaning products or foods (Americans are big on Lemon Pledge, the Brits can't find a decent sausage outside of the UK). Shit, you have to drive on the other side of the road?! Have you and your spouse just made the worst decision of your lives?

Phase Two: The Glass is Half Full

It can take a few months to even begin to settle into a new home, let alone a new country and a new culture. Usually after the repeated questioning of your sanity fades, the initial apprehension and second guessing give way to acceptance. In my experience, acceptance can go one of two ways: **blind optimism or acute homesickness.**

Blind optimism leads you down the garden path in rose-tinted glasses. Everything is awesome. You cling to those silver linings as if your life depended on it. The ground beef tastes funny? No biggie, the pork is great! And cheap! Six months of winter? It makes you appreciate the sunny days all that much more! Thermometer regularly climbing above 115 degrees? Think of all that beach time!

The path of **acute homesickness** is defined by what is missing. The food is different, the people are different, the weather is different. Unlike the blind optimist, the expat suffering from acute homesickness sees *only* the negative. Things are not like they are at home; things at home are so much better. Life is not the same without Lemon Pledge or English sausages.

Neither path is maintainable for long. By seeing only the good, you risk your whole existence falling apart the first time the internet goes down and you have to machete your way through foreign red tape. Conversely, by seeing only the negative, you are missing out on a lot of great stuff. Surely Lemon Pledge is bad for the environment anyway.

Phase Three: Warrior Pose

They say it takes at least a year to settle in anywhere new. Usually by the end of the first year in a new place, the twain has met and some semblance of balance is achieved. This far in, you've likely learned your way around and gained confidence. You may have picked up a little of the lingo, or be well on your way to fluency. You know the route to and from the local Ikea. The head-scratching local customs don't throw you as much. You know, for instance, that you will get a tut and glare if you don't put the little spacer bar between your items and the next person's on the checkout belt or if you don't park with two wheels on the sidewalk so that other cars can pass. You're on the upswing now!

Phase Four: You Reap What You Sow

You've found acceptable substitutes. You've made friends. Your kids are thriving. You can see clearly now the rain has gone. This is the time when you get to reap what you've sown. This is the phase when you realize you need to start taking advantage. Maybe you're an accompanying spouse and you've been able to stop working and spend time with the kids. Maybe you are able to focus your energy on getting fit or doing something creative, learning a new language or skill, *writing a novel*. Maybe you're the working partner and taking that leap of faith is finally starting to pay off. Maybe you get to live in a house, live near the beach, live near the mountains. Maybe your kids get to go to a private school, or you get to ski every weekend, or—and this is the one that usually gets you in the end—maybe you get to travel to places you never would have dreamed of going had you been at home. Oh, the places you'll go!

Phase 5: The Silver Lining Starts to Tarnish

You've established yourself in a community, you feel pretty comfortable navigating the supermarket or dealing with another country's propensity for rules—or lack thereof. You may even be able to offer advice to newbies. You have nice friends, a nice social circle, a nice life. This is usually when the silver linings start to tarnish a bit. Maybe it's financial, maybe it's cultural. Maybe it's just general weariness that your kid is always doing something that is offensive to your host culture. I don't think it's a coincidence that this stage usually coincides with the expat exodus that happens around the two-year mark. Contracts often run on two to three years cycles and once you hit that mark, the departures start to hit closer to home. All of a sudden you start to remember the things you didn't like in the beginning. You start to find new faults, start to distance yourself just a little bit. Maybe you *accidentally* forget to put the little spacer down on the grocery conveyor belt, *just because you can.*

Phase Six: Life is Like a Mixed Tape

Eventually, it's your turn to move. The contract gets signed, the movers come in. Suddenly you remember all the things you said you wanted to do in your host country and didn't get the chance to do. You remember all the things you wanted to buy, all the restaurants you wanted to eat at, the museums you wanted to tour, the trips you wanted to take. Often there's a feeding frenzy of activity, cramming in as much as you can. For some there is the joy of going home, for others the excitement of starting a new adventure, but always tinged with the sadness of saying goodbye to a special kind of friend—one that knows what the circle of expat life is really like. This phase involves a lot of alcohol, a lot of tears and the somewhat humbling realization that you'll soon be starting all over again.

Phase Seven: The Grass is Always Greener

There have only been a handful of expats I've spoken to that didn't have at least a few good things to say about places they had been posted, even if they needed time and distance between them to see it. Whether it was the travel or the perks or the people they met, whether it was the chance for their children to attend a better school, grow up in a safer environment or simply affordable household help, most of us look back with some fondness on the places we've called home, albeit temporarily. These bouts of nostalgia undoubtedly hit when you find yourself navigating the too narrow aisles of a new supermarket or you are begging your friends from the US to send you cans of Goya black beans, when you can't find decent ground beef or you're watching the thermometer plummet. While you wonder if you've made the right decision, if the kids are going to adjust, if you're ever going to find something which will leave your wood furniture citrus fresh and shiny, you find yourself back at the beginning.

It's the circle of expat life.

If you listen closely, sometimes you can hear the strains of a muzak version of Hakuna Matata along the way.

LAST SUPPER (noun):

The final meal you have in a place you've called home for a period of time, often eaten with mixed emotions.

As in: *I sure won't miss the crazy-ass driving or the parking on the sidewalk, but you can't beat a good souvlaki.*

Wine and Cheese (Definitions)

THE IRRATIONAL ANGER OF THE EXPAT SPOUSE
2016

"Irrational angry expat spouse mode isn't fair and it's not even productive. But it's real. And it happens."

I barked at my husband this morning.

More than once.

He didn't do anything. He hadn't said anything or implied anything. He was just reading his book.

Yet I was angry at him because *he was there* and *we are here.*

Sometimes as an expat spouse you find yourself in situations you have no control over. Most of the time your spouse has zero control either, but that just shores up the irrational part of the title. You find yourself in a state of confusion and delay and while there are lots of states that are nice to visit (might I suggest Rhode Island, oft overlooked), confusion and delay is not a nice state to spend any time in.

So you blame your spouse.

They get the blame for no other reason than it's their fault you are here. Or there. Or waiting to decide whether you are here. Or there.

It's their stupid job, their stupid company, their stupid rules and regulations. If it weren't for their stupidness you'd be cooking up vast pots of Goya black beans you bought at Target complaining about that guy in your neighborhood who just *seems* like an asshole.

But you're not, because you're somewhere else. Because of their stupid job.

My husband works for the World Health Organization. You'd think we'd have the best medical care and coverage and insurance ever, right? You'd think we'd be getting MRIs and biopsies with the vitamins. But nope. We have suck ass health insurance. I get infuriated about it even though it's not my husband's fault. But when I get into irrational angry expat wife mode, it's his fault because...well, we're here because of his stupid job.

(In irrational angry expat spouse mode, the benefits don't get a look-see. Irrational, remember?)

A close friend confided that while she and her spouse were deciding between two job offers she was inclined to let her husband make the final decision, not because she didn't care, but so that she could hold him responsible if it all went wrong. She didn't mean it of course, and the decision was made by both of them. But still...

I get it.

His stupid job. Hers. Yours. Whatever. It's his/her/their fault you are here. Or there. Or somewhere in between.

As an expat spouse you get very little say in the way things work. You might have equal say at your own dinner table, in the ultimate decision that takes your family from country to country, but you get no say in things like what health insurance plan is offered or how the pension scheme is set up or how they deal with moving families.

And sometimes the lack of control over even the little things, let alone the big ones, makes you feel cornered. And since most of us can't actively lash out at the companies our spouses work for, we lash out at the next best thing.

Our spouse.

Expat spouses aren't the only ones who feel cornered. But those feelings are amplified when your spouse's regular old stupid job becomes a stupid job in another country.

I've talked to expats who were expected to pick up and move within weeks. Can I explain to you the stress of having to pack up a family and move them to another country, to find schools, a place to live, supermarkets, doctors, dentists, hairdressers, babysitters and a liquor store with a good wine selection in a place there's a good chance you've never even been before?

People do it. That doesn't mean they don't want to brain the head of recruitment at their spouse's company *while* they're doing it. (And since they can't get close enough to the HR guy, their spouse makes a handy understudy.)

I've talked to expats who have been forced to live in different countries because companies don't take into account the difficulty or consequence of moving school children mid-year. Or in their last year of high school. Or the fact there may not be openings. Or housing. Why? Because they don't care or they expect the employee to figure it out, or think throwing money at the problem will fix it. Or they just suck ass.

I haven't met many (if any) expats who felt their spouse's employer did anything to help them or their family adjust to the general trauma of moving. In fact, there is a whole cottage industry of companies who, for a fee, will help you settle into your new home, school, country, etc. (p.s. HR guy, that nice fruit basket doesn't really cover the trauma of packing up and moving three kids and a dog across continental borders, but thanks for the oranges, I guess.)

You know what most companies who hire expats do? Suck. Ass.

Like our health insurance.

Come to think of it, most of these things are pretty rational things to get angry about. But not at my spouse.

Irrational angry expat spouse mode isn't fair and it's not even productive. But it's real. And it happens.

Don't worry too much about my husband. He went back to reading his book. **And I still brought him coffee,** so he knew it was ok. Only *rational* angry expat spouse would deny him coffee.

And she's a bitch.

PRO TIP

Don't worry about finding a BFF, concentrate on the Fs!

Remember those girls you hated in high school? The ones that hated you right back? There is a good chance they are going to be your new best friends.

When you are thrown together into a new and confusing environment, everyone is starting off on equal footing. You'll meet people who wouldn't have given you the time of day way back when. Maybe you even looked down your punk rock nose at them as well. Doesn't matter. A lot of times you won't have anything in common other than the fact you're in the same place at the same time. But just like new moms love to tell stories of labor pains and stitches, expats trade stories and information. Make friends with everyone and anyone. You may not meet your BFF in that first year, but you'll be less lonely. And you never know, you may find out they actually *did* like you way back in high school, but were just too scared of your mohawk to let you know.

HOW TO TELL AN EXPAT IS MOVING
2016

"Most of us become fairly attuned to the little things which often indicate a move before the cute little Paperless Post "We're Moving" announcement hits your inbox."

Here in the global village of ExpatLandia, there is often a prescribed way to say goodbye. There are parties and coffees and more parties and lots of cake. Champagne flows pretty freely, even during the day. Books are signed and monies collected. Gifts bought. I'm sure it varies from place to place, but there's a pattern which is almost formulaic.

I've been here long enough to know Jo will bring the mackerel pate, Jill the avocado dip and Marta will buy something five minutes before she needs to be wherever she needs to be. It lends a bit of comfort to what can be an unsettling feeling. After all, it's never easy to say goodbye, no matter how many times you do it.

All of that, however, only begins once a family has officially announced their move. For contractual reasons or just personal ones, sometimes people keep a new posting under wraps until the last possible minute. Still, most of us become fairly attuned to the little things which indicate a move before the cute little Paperless Post "We're Moving" announcement hits your inbox.

Here are ten to watch out for:

—The donations, hand-me-downs and small items start to appear on bulletin boards, list-serves and flea market pages. Once the appliances start to get listed, you can assume the contract's been signed.
–The car goes in for an overhaul and tune up, the tires changed and all the dings and scratches get fixed.

—All the freezer meals come out in a last-ditch effort to get rid of the meat bought on sale, the bolognese sauce from six months ago, and the turkey the company doled out as a bonus last Christmas.

—You go a casual dinner and your host's **entire bar** is on display. They eagerly encourage you to drink cocktails made with rum or tequila and try to foist the unopened bottle of créme de menthe on you.

—They start going to museums and concerts and walking tours, 'exploring' the city, all things which they haven't gotten around to in the previous three years.

—They start to get a bit cagey about planning future dates and won't commit to anything beyond the end of the school year beyond "we'll see".

—The "I have a friend looking for information about schools in Bangkok" posts start to pop up on your Facebook feed.

—They start to withdraw from their normal social scene.

—They start to take more local vacations and trips than usual.

—Conversations are suddenly full of all things they love about where they are or conversely, all the dislikes are dragged out and rehashed.

Some of these things are necessities, after all, no one wants to waste the booze the movers won't pack. Others, like withdrawing a bit from friendships, even close ones, is often a way to buffer the mixed feelings most of us have about moving on. Expats on the go, or on deck to go, will seek out anything that will make a time of massive upheaval feel just a little bit easier.

So while the rest of us wait for the official announcement on Facebook or the ping of a Paperless Post announcement, rest assured. Jo's already got her mackerel paté ready. The bubbles are chilling. And we've been collecting money for your book and Royal Copenhagen mugs as soon as we saw you list your washer/dryer set for sale.

EXPAT ENNUI (noun):

Feeling like you've done the sights, sampled the cuisine, toured the museums and are posted out.

As in: *Oh God, not the Little Mermaid again.*

Wine and Cheese (Definitions)

THE MAGIC QUILT OF EXPAT LIFE
2018

"Saying goodbye is hard. We should cry. And laugh. And rejoice and give thanks and feel sad. This is the reality of our life."

I've been an expat for nearly ten years. Blimey, that's a long time; long enough to start using the word blimey in a non-ironic way, even. Nearly ten years overseas means I have said more than my fair share of goodbyes. I've gone to a lot of leaving lunches, farewell festivities, and tally-ho teas. I've drunk kegs full of coffee, ingested numerous kilos of cake and watched the resulting kilos materialize on my ass. I've given speeches, listened to speeches, presented gifts, bought gifts, assembled slide shows, written songs.

I've done it all.

It never gets any easier, not really. I almost always cry.

Not big, gulping sobs, though sometimes it has come close. But that sort of crying when you can feel it coming down the track: the tight throat, the sting behind your eyes, the stuffed up nose. It bears down upon you like a freight train and there's little you can do to get out of the way in time. A whistle of warning, someone choking on a word, and that's all she wrote, folks.

A room full of weepy women.

I wrote a long time ago about the importance of *not* crying during these things. Five years later I've changed my mind.

Cry, cry, cry. Cry a river if you need to. It's good for the soul. More people should cry, and more often.

Newsflash: Women cry. We cry when we're happy. When we're sad. When we are frustrated or overwhelmed or raging like a menopausal witch. (No? Just me?) We cry over car commercials and Christmas commercials, during movies and reading books. We cry when someone else's kid's feelings get hurt. We cry at the very *idea* of something happening to someone we know. We cry when we meet our family at the airport, when they leave, when we fight with our partners, when our kids say something hurtful. We cry as we watch our kids walk across a graduation stage, when someone else's baby is born, when things go awry.

We cry.

So, when you get a room full of women in a room, women who've spent a few years getting to know one another, giving each other rides and acting as emergency contacts, getting to know each other's kids and families, seeing each other through difficulties, partners working in other countries, all clinging together for dear life on this life boat of friendship in a foreign land–when you get a room full of women like that together and someone gets choked up? You almost always end up with a room full of weepy women.

These ritual goodbyes and all the emotions they evoke is a kind of exquisite torture. It's incredibly poignant to hear stories and reminiscences, to look at years worth of pictures, to see the evolution of friendships play out in celluloid. It's like watching a time-lapse of a child growing up.

I've been tasked with putting together a few of these slide shows. When I do, I always include a montage of people who have already said goodbye, though it's becoming increasingly difficult for me to remember whose paths have crisscrossed after this many years, whose lives have become entangled with whose. But I do it so that those folks, the ones we've already said goodbye to, remain a part of the whole. A panel that when stitched together with all of the others makes a quilt of a certain time and place.

The best part? It's a magic quilt which keeps growing.

Saying goodbye *is* hard. We should cry. And laugh. And rejoice and give thanks and feel sad. This is the reality of our life. Sometimes it can seem like a life abroad is glamorous vacations and non-stop parties, but the edges of a life lived outside the borders of your own country can be rough. It's just that no one takes photos of all those tears, those rooms full of weepy women, and posts them up on Facebook.

But maybe we should.

As a storyteller, it's an incredible privilege to hear the stories that belong to others. As a human being, and a friend, it's humbling when I get to be a **part** of that story. A panel on someone else's quilt.

So many times those stories start off with feelings of loneliness and isolation, feeling stranded and out-of-place, nervous, unsure footing on choppy seas that are taking you far from everything you know. And then the magic: one day, one coffee, one conversation, one friend. The tide begins to turn. The seas calm. You look around, and far from being alone, you're at a table for forty eating kilos of cake.

Just look how it ends: a room full of twenty, thirty, forty, sixty people who have put aside a chunk of their day to celebrate a friend, a friendship, to say goodbye and good luck. It ends in a room full of women to whom you mean enough that they hold back a tear, wipe a wizened eye, choke back a sob. A panel on that magic expat quilt that never stops growing.

Just look what you mean.

Blimey, indeed.

PRO TIP

Enjoy it while it lasts!

Some families have signed up for a lifetime of this nomadic lifestyle, but others do so for a limited time: a year's sabbatical, a two-year contract. Whatever your frame, enjoy your time. You are getting the chance of a lifetime to immerse yourself in a new country, a new culture, to see new places, learn new things, reinvent yourself. Make the most of it. Someday you may even look back and laugh at having had all those people up your ass the whole time.

BITTERSWEET'S NOT JUST FOR CHOCOLATE
2012

"If it truly does take a village, what do you do when you're half a world away from home?"

Remember the airport scene at the end of *Love, Actually*? The one with the montage of lovers and families reuniting at Heathrow–the general air of excitement and joy and even a few tears set to a melodic Beach Boys soundtrack? Well, when you live a long distance flight from your family, it's quite possible you've actually lived this scene. Perhaps more than once. Maybe without the music though. Or Alan Rickman.

What the producers *don't* show you is the flip-side–the return flight. When you lug moms and dads and siblings and luggage back to the airport at the end of another visit and leave them there, returning all by your lonesome.

There are great things about living in another country. There are even good things about not living in the same country as your family (no surprise visits when you are hungover and ignoring your kids and your laundry hasn't been done in a few weeks, fewer well-meant suggestions....) But there are downsides too. And often, particularly when you've just said goodbye, the scale tips massively in favor of the downs.

The bittersweetness of the family visit.

We have always lived at least an ocean apart from one family or another. We've become adept at navigating the perils of holiday time-shares and experienced the utter joy of hauling children, gifts, and ourselves through airports during the Christmas season. Thanksgiving–that most wonderful, secular American holiday was a God-send as it's only an American thing. But now that we live overseas, it's a thing of the past.

My kids are the only grandchildren on my side. And we live nearly 4,000 miles away. Guilt, is that you? My mother also has the misfortune of living in a neighborhood where many extended families have chosen to live together–old world style–adding on to houses, living above, building around the corner. She is surrounded by OPG: Other People's Grandchildren. And while she would never tell me how much it hurts, or how jealous she is, I am neither blind, obtuse, or dumb. When she sees my kids, they've grown three inches and are learning another language. They've completed six months of another grade, taken up a new sport, joined four new clubs and don't like the same toys they did the last time. Like a lot of expat families, we spend summers at 'home', so my mother and sister get to spend larger chunks of time with the kids than they would if we lived closer, but I won't kid myself into thinking it's a substitute for cheering them on at a sports match or coming to a birthday party or watching them wake up on Christmas morning.

Then there are the selfish things, like the fact that free babysitting is only a forlorn fantasy. When you live in a place where importance is placed on family (and it certainly is in Denmark, as it was in Cyprus), you can get a bit lonely when it's just the small family unit– over and over and over again. Family time is overrated when it's *all family, all the time*. There's no watching a football game with a beer while Granny chases after the kids, no *Mom can you come and help because the kids and I are playing vomit roulette and I need someone to take care of me as well*. No cheeky overnights away with your spouse to catch up on sleep. No two a.m. panicked phone calls trying to figure out why your baby has a fever hot enough to fry an egg.

Extended families miss out on the everyday–the funny things my little one says, the perfect score the older one comes home with on his math homework. You store them up for Skype chats and weekly phone calls, but most of it slips through the cracks. Add a time difference that puts you on different sides of the AM/PM divide and it gets even harder.

When politicians are elected, they spend the first year trying to do something and the rest of the time planning their re-election campaign. It's the same with family visits. We spend the first day or two catching up and having fun, and then the rest of the time is spent trying to figure out when the next visit will be. Plotting the graph lines between school vacations, time off from work, and finances takes military precision.

It's great to be instrumental in opening up someone else's eyes to another part of the world, another culture, fantastic sights–places they might never have visited had we not decided to live this upside-down life.

But saying goodbye is always hard.

If it truly does take a village, what do you do when you're half a world away from home?

SPANISH FLU (noun):

What you pretend the whole family has in order to take them out of school a few days early to avoid the 200% airfare increase that is tacked onto school holiday times.

As in: *We're flying to Barcelona two days before school breaks up. Cough, cough.*

Wine and Cheese (Definitions)

THE WEIGHT OF (MOVING AROUND) THE WORLD ON YOUR SHOULDERS
2016

"Is it any wonder expats seem to drink as much as they do?"

I've written a lot about life as an expat, but always through the window of my own experience: that of the non-earning partner.

It's not often I try to put myself in the shoes of the one whose job brings you to another country, whose carefully negotiated package determines everything from where you live to how many times a year you get to go home. The one upon whose shoulders rests the weight of the world, quite literally at times.

We first packed up and moved with the peacekeeping arm of the United Nations. We bypassed all the shit postings you often have to get your feet mucky in on the UN circuit. We skipped the war zones and zipped past the just-finished war zones. We circumvented the countries without stable governments and landed, pretty softly, in what's generally considered the cherry on top of the whipped cream atop the UN peacekeeping cake: Cyprus.

I hated it, at least for the first year. I hated it so vehemently and vociferously that it became a running joke at my husband's office, where they would often greet new staff with a variation of the following:

Welcome to Cyprus, the posting everyone's trying to get into, expect for Dina, who's trying to leave.

I was so far up my own ass for those first twelve months it took me a long time to realize how my unhappiness was eating away at my spouse, who had quietly assumed responsibility for my misery. It wasn't a question of letting him as much as not being aware it was happening.

Yes, my head was that far up my ass.

There's plenty of guilt I carry with me, but not the guilt, worry, and stress shouldered by the one responsible for pin-balling a family around the globe. My go-to joke is that starting work in a new country means a new office, a new cafeteria, and maybe a new stapler if you're lucky. That's oversimplified, of course. Getting used to working in a new environment with new colleagues can be terribly stressful. Add in a spouse who is unhappy, kids who are crying because they miss their friends and eating unknown cuts of meat every night and well, is it any wonder expats seem to drink as much as they do?

Good friends who moved recently tallied the stress levels involved in picking your family up and repositioning them around the globe. Three months of packing up/leaving/worrying stress on the old end followed by three months of unpacking/settling in/worrying stress on the new one.

Six months of feeling unsettled and a lot of the time, unhappy. If you move every two years, that's a quarter of your life navigating the sea of stress with nothing but a flight home to paddle your way upstream.

That's a lot of stress. It's not good for your heart. Or your marriage. Or your liver if you self-medicate with wine.

I've joked (and been serious about) the anger some feel toward the working partner, most often as a handy stand-in for companies who like to toss employees around the world like rag dolls. But I've never really stopped to think about what it's like to be the one on the receiving end of that anger or unhappiness and how much it must affect the quality of *their* life.

Though we generally don't have to worry about cutbacks and layoffs as much as some (chalk one up for the UN: there's never any shortage of war or disease), it's a legitimate and sobering worry for others.

Copenhagen is a hub for the oil industry, which is experiencing major cut-backs and lay-offs and *sayonara, we can't afford you* anymores. We've watched families step off the plane and get turned back around with a package and a pat on the back. Others have been made redundant just as they were settling in. Some have been here for years, consider it home and suddenly? They're out of a job.

Obviously losing your job sucks whether you're an expat or not, but the added of stress of losing your job, or potentially losing your job, when you've carted your entire family overseas adds a whole new dimension.

Sometimes it's the hard-to-shake worry you've made the wrong decision. Feeling as if a major decision rests squarely on your shoulders, combined with watching your partner and kids struggle to settle--those things are huge. To bear responsibility on one set of shoulders is enormous. And usually, unfair.

As much as I like to wax on/wax off about our crappy health insurance or paint the fence with the layers of common sense which are sorely lacking when it comes to expecting families to move around the world in eight days, the sole responsibility should not be placed at my husband's feet or on his shoulders, regardless of how broad they may be.

We are partners: in marriage, in parenting, in the topsy-turvy world of living outside our countries. We went into this beautiful mess together and we'll shoulder the responsibility together. In the nearly eight years we've been doing this, I've pulled my head out of my ass long enough to see that.

If Atlas shrugs, shaking us from one continent to the next, we'll shoulder the weight together.

PRO TIP

Always Count Your Change!

This one is especially true for American expats, for whom the highest denomination of coinage is a measly $0.25. I don't think it's even enough to make a phone call any more. But in lots of other places, those coins add up. In Denmark, you get coins up to 20 DKK. That's almost $3.50. Practically half a cup of coffee! So don't ignore the shrapnel. Save up enough of it, you may be able to buy your friends a cup of coffee too!

TURNING TO FACE THE STRANGE
2016

"This is the gift that moving has taught me: nothing has to be forever."

Sitting with a good friend who is soon to be repatriating, we zipped our way up and down the standardized questions:

Are you going back to the house you lived in before?

Have you sorted out school for the kids?

How do you **feel**?

As we delicately wove our way through the challenges churned up by any move, we talked a little about her family's willingness to test the repatriation waters to see if the temperature was right before committing to anything permanent.

You know those Homer Simpson **"Doh!"** moments when the light bulb clicks on above your head? I had one of them. Because in her statement, bold as brass, was the truth about the greatest gift I've been given on this topsy-turvy expat journey: the willingness to turn and face the strange.

Seven and a half years ago when my husband brought up the prospect of leaving my beloved NYC, I was more than slightly terrified. The fear stemmed from a multitude of reasons, but the biggest was questioning my ability to successfully move myself, my little nuclear family and our belongings 7,000 miles away from family, friends and take-out. The plan was to stay out in the field for two to three years. Two turned to four, then six, now here we are going into our eighth.

Even though moving again is a near certainty, even though I know it will be one giant pain in the ass, I no longer doubt I can do it. The time we've spent abroad has taught me that nothing is permanent, and I mean that in the best way possible.

I've loosened up. Sure, I still like a good spreadsheet. I still like plans A through F lined up like ducks in a row. But our time as expats has taught me that if one way doesn't work, there's sure to be another one that does. I've learned to accept the change, to face the strange.

As my own life get ever so closer to words like pension and retirement and further from ones like boozy brunch, we will be faced with certain decisions. Seven years ago, those decisions may well have paralyzed me into indecision. Even three years ago. But the longer we're out, the more clear it becomes that everything doesn't need to be clear, not immediately anyway.

I wouldn't call our life nomadic, we are rooted to a large degree, but living outside our comfort zone has, strangely, only widened the zone in which I feel comfortable. I think most expats feel the same.

This is the gift that moving has taught me: nothing has to be forever. Change is not to be feared. If it isn't working, we'll pick up and find a way to make it work. I'm not saying it won't be uncomfortable or scary. It will almost certainly be stressful and anxiety provoking. I mean I don't feel like we have to lock ourselves into a decision that is forever and ever until death do us part.

On the surface it doesn't sound like a big thing, but stop for a minute and think about all the things fear of change may have stopped you from doing–quitting a dead-end job, leaving a deader-ender relationship, moving, even trying a new dish at your favorite restaurant. Our time as expats has taught me the importance of flexibility as well as the courage to face change.

When our second son was born, we named him Reed. One of the very first comments someone made to me was how wonderful it was to be named after a part of nature which has the ability to bend and sway with whichever way the wind changes, but never lose its strength. It's a characteristic I think many of us discover on our journeys, and one in which I am only now truly learning to appreciate.

Here's hoping it's one I can remember for a long time to come. Maybe even over a boozy brunch in a place I never thought I'd find myself.

EXPAT SPEAK

Q: Where did you move from? (Note: this is an entirely different than asking where you come from)

Translation: Is this your first overseas stint? The answer dictates which way the conversation will shift. This question is like the fork in the conversational road. Talk will either shift onto the path of 'how can I help you?' or onto the road of 'let's compare places we've lived'.

NINE MORE EXPATS YOU'LL MEET ABROAD
2017

Victoria the Veteran

Victoria has seen generations of expats come...and go. She's been around long enough that she's practically part of the furniture. She knows her way around, navigating not only the place, but the relationships that make up the place. Vic has ten different toes dipped in ten different circles–because she knows just how fleeting expat friendships can be. Some think she's ice-cold because the constant goodbyes don't seem to faze her, but it's more that years on the scene have hardened her to goodbyes....just a little.

Freak-out Frannie.

Frannie finds it hard to breathe deep and relax no matter how many hot yoga classes she signs up for. It doesn't matter how smooth things seem to be going, there's always cause for a freak-out. If it's not the math curriculum, it's the school lunches. Or something on the news. Or the cost of living. Or the way the traffic light doesn't give you enough time to cross the street. The local propensity for liberally dropping the f-bomb into conversation sends her into convulsions. Her heart's in the right place–it's just always beating too fast, set to semi-permanent panic mode.

Homesick Harriet

Harry gets monthly parcels sent from home, keeps up all her magazine subscriptions at exorbitant prices, and subscribes to whatever local cable package that lets her watch her favorite shows. She travels home at every given opportunity and brings food back in her luggage. She shops online–from stores in her own country. **First-year Freyas** are usually half-Harriet by default, but true Harriets never really embrace living abroad. They always have one foot where they're living and another one firmly planted at home.

Traveling Tony

It's a stretch to call Tony an expat, as he's usually not in town long enough to sleep in his own bed more than three nights in a row. Tony usually heads up family of 'lifeboat expats'–women and children only– who stay behind in one place while he plies his trade all over the globe. Sometimes it's hard for Tony's spouse to convince others he actually exists. Perhaps those wedding photos you see when you go to their amazingly furnished house are just props after all?

Never-Going-Back Niamh

Like many expats, Niamh was skeptical at first, but took to expat life like a fish outta the Atlantic and relocated to the Pacific. So much so that Niamh never plans on going back home. Ever. In fact, Niamh will do anything, including moving internationally three times in a year, just to avoid it. Whether it's the life, the opportunities, or the bonds, Niamh has embraced life as expat to the fullest extent and you'll have to pry it out of her cold, dead hands.

Repatriating Rena

While Niamh settles in for a life of transient relocation, Rena is getting ready to move home and experiencing the nausea of the repatriation rollercoaster. Whether she's been gone one year or ten, life outside has made her question what life will be like back 'inside'. Will she re-fit in? Will her kids be ok? Rena's worries often gets lost in the two-step expat shuffle because people assume going home is easier....but as Rena worries, it may be anything but.

Pam the Polyglot

A round in Russian? Да! A stint in Shang-hai? 好! A post in Paraguay? Si! Pam picks up the local language wherever she lands–and not just enough to order a coffee and a cup of the Bolshoi borscht. Pam can carry on conversations with the locals, understand and answer when folks stop her on the street, and get around by taxi no problem. Pam's linguistic gymnastics often make her English-speaking compatriots feel guilty for not trying harder-the ones who rely solely on their mother tongue to get by without making much of an effort beyond nej, tak...

Superiority Complex Sam

Sam never has a good word to say about the place she's landed. Not one. Oh sure, there's nothing an expat coffee klatch likes more than a little bitch about little annoyances and cultural quirks, but Sam's insults take a much broader focus. There's *nothing* about her adopted country that suits her, *everything* is better where she comes from.

Fay the Fantasy

Fay is the expat we all aspire to be...and fail miserably at. The one who settles in with ease. Who speaks the language within months. Who has no trouble finding the expensive cheese she likes at the market in Uruguay that doesn't even sell cheese. She travels extensively, her kids are involved in local sports programs, and she still Skypes her family back home twice a week. She takes every shock that a new culture sends up her spine with a smile and can pack up her family and move at the drop of a hat. With grace. Fay doesn't really exist outside our collective expat imagination–but it doesn't stop us from wanting to be her anyway.

SUPERMARKET SWEEP (noun):

The act of going up and down the aisle of a foreign supermarket numerous times looking for something...then finding it the place you'd least expect.

As in: Why on Earth would the peanut butter be with the pasta products?

Wine and Cheese (Definitions)

FOUR EXPATS AND A FUNERAL
2014

"When you make a friend as an expat, you slice through the niceties."

When you live abroad and someone on the other side of the world is gravely ill or passes away, normal rules don't apply. No one pops round with a tuna casserole to help the family out. There is no Shiva sitting or sympathy cards with the promise of masses held on the behalf of the deceased. Despite the lack of what may normally be expected–the food, the family, the familiar– there *is* an understanding.

There is rallying of a different sort.

When I had to travel to a funeral in the U.S. not too long ago, no one brought me a lasagna. Instead I had friends offer to watch my kids while I flew across the Atlantic. I had other friends offer to make their lunches, pick them up in the morning, take them home after school if my husband needed to be at work. As yummy as a chicken pot pie might be, as traditional as sitting with the bereaved may seem, when you are an expat, the offers of help with the everyday, the standing in for family, those things mean far more.

You might be reading this thinking, *that doesn't seem so out of the ordinary.* What you must remember, however, is that these are not life long friends. This isn't Jodie from high school who saw me puke my schnapps up or Sandy from college who lied to my parents about where I'd been the night before. This isn't Julie, neighbor of fifteen years or Sue the woman I've known since Mommy and Me music class. These are people who, on the timeline of life, I've really only just met.

That's the thing about expat friendships. The analogy I come back to over and over again is that expat friendships happen in dog years. When you make a friend as an expat, you slice through the niceties. You dice through the *getting to know you* phase. Normal time is compressed, allowing you to get closer faster than you normally would. Whereas maybe you saw Sue every Wednesday morning at nine when you rolled your eyes singing *The Hokey Pokey*, expat friends are often present in every nook and cranny of your life abroad. They are de-facto family as well as friends. They make up your community as well as your social life. They are kith, kin, village and vicar. They are who you turn to for advice, for an ear to listen, a shoulder to cry on. They are the ones who listen to you vent and more importantly, understand, because they are right there with you. And because they are there all the time, not just on the end of a messenger chat or a signature at the bottom of a Christmas card, it truly feels like you've known them just as long as Jodie or Sandy or even cousin Jane who used to cover for you when you fed scraps of food to the potted plant at Great Aunt Edna's house.

There is an intensity to expat friendship that reminds me of the friendships of middle school, when the sun rose and set with the movements of your best friend. There is a camaraderie about expat friendship which makes me think of the first mom friend you made after the birth of your first child, when you heaved a sigh of relief you had found someone who wouldn't roll their eyes if you discussed poop colors. There is the free fall experience of falling in love thrown in as well, a sudden need and desire to unburden your secrets and fears, though you've only just met. I've told expat friends who I've known for mere minutes things that friends I've had since high school don't know.

There is a bond, a togetherness, a Band of Brothers-esque sense of getting each other's back. I've looked after someone else's child for a weekend so her parents could escape for some well needed time together, something I can't imagine doing for more than one or two people in 'real life'. I have had countless others offer to take my own kids so that my husband and I can get away. I've hugged people I don't know very well upon hearing about the death of a loved one across another ocean or ten countries away. I have listened in as others have planned, with military precision, how to organize meals and child care and dog walking for a fellow expat going through chemo.

These are relationships based upon the bedrock of a shared experience, a profound experience that for a time, defines everything about you. I have been a part of this shared experience, have witnessed the compressed, intense bonding of these relationships, both in myself and in others. Necessity compels you to disregard all the small, quirky things that would normally prevent you from being friends in some other reality, some parallel universe. Sometimes you dispense with the big things as well. Of course not all expats are friends with one another simply because they are in the same place at the same time. It's not as if everyone gets naked and frolics in the hot tub of life abroad. Far from it. There are cliques and groups and people who don't like each other with an intensity bordering on manic–in other words, it's just like real life–the one outside the expat bubble. What *is* different is the closeness you feel to those you do like–and the speed at which that closeness develops.

These distilled friendship are one of the best parts of living abroad. They are relationships filtered through cheesecloth. They are sifted and sieved until you are left with the simple core: a mutual admiration and respect for the person sitting across from you. The one offering to look after your kids or walk your dog or pop in and feed your guinea pigs while you are gone.

I was only away for a few days. The house was still upright when I got back. The boys had been fed and watered, nothing was broken, homework had been done. This time I didn't have need for the assistance of my little village, but there will eventually be a time when I do, when I need to reach out and ask for the type of help I wouldn't dream of asking of another kind of friend.

I won't hesitate because I know they will say yes, the same way that I would, that I do.

PRO TIP

Streamline sentimentality!

Virgo neurosis aside, when you are moving from place to place every few years, you become very picky about what stays and what goes. In our marriage, my husband is the more sentimental of the two. While I long for the day when I can decorate like a grown up with breakable objects and without having to step over boxes of trucks and bins of color-coded Lego, he gets slightly misty when it comes time to cull the boys' things. I have saved a few favorite books, tee shirts that tell a story, but everything else gets donated, given away, or sold. Harsh maybe, but a necessity when you are charged by the cubic foot and you don't have a basement.

SHOW ME THE WAY TO GO HOME
2015

"I worry that moving back to what I've always viewed as home is going to be just as much of a shock to the system as moving abroad was, yet without the support network."

When I traveled back to Denmark in November after my grandmother's funeral, I was carrying some extra weight with me. A little extra cushioning below the belt, a suitcase full of brown paper craft bags (don't ask), a few new books and a tiny seed of longing to move home tucked in a side pocket.

Funerals are emotional affairs under any circumstance. I'm sure that heightened sense of emotion played a part in returning home to Copenhagen with a mild fever of homesickness. Yet standing there, a giantess among my very short Italian family, I felt like I was back among my people. Even if I did have to bend at the knees to greet most of them. The loudness, the chewing with the mouth open, the jokes bordering on inappropriate–all of that is as familiar to me as the freckles on my face. It felt normal to me. It felt comforting. It felt like *home*.

There is a strange sense of weightlessness when you come **home** after being *home*. For a few hours or a few days, you are caught between the here and now, the now and then, the then and there. It's like emotional jet-lag, when there are bits and pieces of your heart in two places at once.

Normally, by the time you unpack, by the time you get the seventy-two loads of laundry underway, and after a good night's sleep in your own bed, you can shake off the feeling of having your head in one time zone and your heart in another. Maybe it was the physical reminders I chose to take, a few sentimental items of my Nana's. Maybe it was the photographs I took with me. Hell, maybe it was the craft bags. But this time there was a palpable, identifiable yearning waiting for me in between the clothes and the books and the toiletries as I unpacked.

It's the first time in a long time I've felt a pull to go home. We are happy here in Denmark. Sure, we know it's not a forever home. We know that as the calendar months turn over into years, we're getting to a point on our timeline when we have to start making plans for the future. So in a way, it was nice to feel that small embryo of "I'm ready to go back home." And yet..

And yet...I fear I don't know the way home. The longer we are away, the further the idea of 'home' slips from my grasp until I am sometimes afraid I won't be able to find my way back.

A lot has changed. Neighborhoods have changed so that I don't recognize them. The slang is different, favorite restaurants have closed, there are suddenly ubiquitous chain restaurants that didn't exist when we left. Friends have dispersed, kids have grown up. There have been massive cultural shifts. But more than anything else, I have changed.

I worry. I worry about fitting in at home, something I've never even given a thought to in the past. I worry about being 'other' in a place where I should be firmly planted in the 'us' camp. I worry I've missed out on cult television shows. I worry I won't get the references, get the jokes. I worry I will laugh when people complain about the cost of things because hell, a hamburger costs $20 here. I worry my kids will have missed out on those sticky early years when friendships are cemented in place.

I worry that moving back to what I've always viewed as home is going to be just as much of a shock to the system as moving abroad was, yet without the support network. No one thinks you need a support network when you're moving where everybody knows your name. Yet I have a sneaking suspicion that's when you need it the most.

Still, within the uncertainty is also the promise of roots, the promise of the familiar, the promise of a little bit more breathing room. It is the promise of returning from a stupendously, fabulously, every-second-instagram-worthy adventure and falling into your own bed for the first time in ages. The one that is molded to your shape, the one that's not too hard or too soft but is just right. There is a gravitational pull toward the familiar I think many of us carry with us, a deep-rooted longing to be home.

I would guess that many of us are also afraid we've forgotten how to go back there.

For now, we have no immediate plans to sort and pack and call up the shipping company. But the time is coming, I can see it out there on the horizon. Whether or not it's this move or the next, eventually we will return to what I've always, in the back of my mind, considered home. I fervently hope that my short, Italian tribe will still be in abundance and that my exceedingly tall husband and soon to be exceedingly tall children will have the opportunity to bend at the knees to hug them. I hope when the time comes, I have someone to help show me the way back.

Most of all I hope that if or when we return, we will feel that our time away has not been too long or too short, but like that bowl full of porridge, just right.

We can never replace the friends who are leaving, even if new bodies fill their spots at the table. Even if the new bodies become friends. Even if the acquaintances we have now become more than that. It won't be the same. It doesn't mean it can't be as good or even better, but it won't be the same.

Expats talk a lot about the ones leaving, the difficulties of re-settling, of finding new friends in a new place. What we very rarely talk about is being left behind and making new friends in the old place.

It's like the age-old question of the chicken and the egg. Is it better to be the one to go, or the last man standing?

SPEED EQUALS DISTANCE OVER TIME
2018

"Every time I watch my mother say goodbye to my kids something small inside me dies."

Living far away from family does funny things to what should otherwise be a straight forward equation. Especially when it comes to speed. And aging.

Yes, I'm quite sure speed gets ramped up when you factor in long-distances and divide them by time spent with family.

I see my mother and sister twice a year. Once here, once there. It's not ideal, but it's more than a lot of expats get, and so for that, I'm thankful. But when family visits are limited to bi-annual hugs and semi-yearly dinners, you notice the passage of time more acutely–etched out on a loved one's face, in the gray of their hair or the stoop of shoulders.

And that's just me.

Each and every time I face it I am slammed with the inevitability of time. And distance. And the speed at which they seem to be colliding.

Time? Time is a wall I keep trying to scale, but instead I keep running into it headfirst, knocking myself most of the way to unconscious. And distance? Well, distance is the one thing in my control.

I don't get homesick very often, not anymore, but I do miss my family. I look forward to their visits, and to mine. In my head I map out great big plans to relax. We'll laugh and have deep conversations and go for long walks! We'll spend quality time! The kids will be gracious and happy to see their family and actually converse with them instead of retreating behind a screen anytime I leave the room!

I worry the reality of those visits is....less than great. Or relaxing. I think I may come across as, for lack of a better word, *grumpy.* Instead of being all hunky and dory, sometimes I get snippy and snappy.

Bear with me. It took me nine long years to figure this out.

I realized I must come across as resentful. Or annoyed. Or just garden variety grumpy-pants. The truth is, there's often an emotional orgy going on in my head, decisions battling reality–decisions which benefit US, but sometimes come at the detriment of extended family.

So when I'm being snippy, it's sometimes because I'm fending off the guilt that come with choosing to live far away. Sometimes when it seems like I'm short-tempered it's because I'm trying to gauge how long I can justify keeping the grandkids away. If it seems like I'm a bit low on patience, it may just be because I'm trying to calculate how much longer I'm going to ask my mother to get on a plane for Christmas. If it seems like I'm sulky, it's probably because I'm trying to remember the formula to figure out how time speeds up when there's a greater distance involved.

I think my brain switches into efficiency mode due to overload. And efficiency mode? Well, everything gets done, but sometimes at the expense of emotion. Al's got nothing on me when I switch over to efficiency mode.

Just ask my husband.

Sure, there's Skype and FaceTime, and it definitely helps, but anyone who lives abroad knows that E.T. was right: phoning home is really just a substitute for being there.

Then the trips are over. Bags are packed, flights checked-in on, passports stamped. It takes me a few weeks to recalibrate my emotions, to pack them all back into the neat boxes they live in. I get caught up in day-to-day dramas and hourly ados and I'll sit down to put my feet up and suddenly it's Sunday, or summer or six months later. And I gear up to do the whole thing all over again.

I'm in the midst of all that now. Long enough removed from the family visit to be able to take a step backward and say "Ah! Of course that's why I was such a miserable Mabel, because I worry about how *our* choice to live away affects *you*. And you're getting older. And I'm getting older. And the kids are getting older. And oh, my God, for the love of all that's holy make it stop!"

Eventually the scales will tip one way or another. But there are few weeks a year when they swing wildly from one side to another, bouncing up and down.

Every time I watch my mother say goodbye to my kids something small inside me dies. Like that flower in ET, the one that wilts and falters. But.... I also know this. You know the final scene of ET? The one when Eliot is crying and Gertie has snot running down her face and ET is about to get on his spaceship? He touches his light-up heart, then points his long, wrinkly finger at Eliot's head and says..."I'll be right here."

It doesn't matter what the formula is for calculating distance, or speed, or even time. Because that's where we are.

We'll be right here.

DIPPING (verb):

From the Danish custom of 'dipping' in the sea, naked, year round.

The act of dipping a toe or another small body part into local custom to get a taste for it.

As in: *I suppose I could get used to curried herring...*

Wine and Cheese (Definitions)

HOW TO MAKE AND KEEP EXPAT FRIENDS
2018

"Losing friends is never easy, no matter how many times you do it. Keeping those friends, especially when they're hopping around the globe, is hard too."

And so another season of goodbyes is upon us. I've written extensively about the art of saying goodbye to good friends. I've walked the walk, talked the talk, and all the rest. Nearly ten years of saying goodbye to acquaintances, friends, good friends, and the ones who feel more like family than friends has left me with lots of feels, many days of runny mascara, and a handful of trite, but true quotes.

Don't cry because it's over, smile because it happened, right?

Dr. Seuss-isms aside, when you get through all the coffees and teas and tears and goodbyes...*then what?*

Set up a group chat. And USE it.
When we started this journey ten years ago, I was a social media neophyte. Facebook you say? Nah, that's for the whippersnappers. What's App? More like What's *That?*

Touching down in Cyprus, little did I know what a huge part Facebook would play in my life.

At any given time, I've got five or six different message groups going. They are the first line of defense in keeping long-distance friendships up and running. There's an ongoing dialogue: who's doing what, who's fed up with their kids, who got a puppy, or a job, or a divorce. It's casual, like meeting for coffee. You can pop in and say hi, let loose with a rant about how your teenager is driving you crazy, or update the group. It works across countries, seasons, and time zones. My only advice is to make sure you're replying to the right group before you hit *return.*

Keep up with the day-to-day

Those Messenger or What's App groups? They're fantastic for keeping up with the day-to-day maintenance of friendship. By sharing the tidbits and highlights, the everyday stuff, there's no pressure to do a massive *"This is what I've been doing for the last year! What about you?"* catchup. And when you do meet up in person, you don't feel like you've missed out–because you've kept each other in the loop.

Understand it won't be the same

When you've moved on or have friends that have, the original bond that held you together, being in the same place at the same time, is broken. You're not experiencing the same endless shitty winter or worries about whether your kid is learning enough math. You may not be bemoaning the cost of a new pair of sneakers or even gossiping about a mutual acquaintance. Your conversations will flow differently because you're experiencing different things. The sameness is now your different-ness. But that doesn't mean the friendship can't or won't survive. Don't fall into the trap of thinking that expat friendships can't–or shouldn't–evolve. They can–and do.

Technology isn't going anywhere so you may as well use it

Skype or FaceTime work great for many expats. I can't stand seeing myself on video (that loose neck skin is *killing me...*) but I have issues, so don't use me as an example. My kids are actually much better at this than I am. Technology allows them to play video games with a friends all over the globe chatting in between blowing shit up. Social media means they don't need to reconnect because they never really disconnected. For all my bitching and moaning about technology, this is the upside. And it's a pretty amazing one.

Make plans

If ten years of expatriation has taught me anything, it is this: the people meant to stay in your life will stay in your life...*as long as you make the effort.* So make the effort. Make plans to see each other. Put aside an annual weekend to get together—and stick to it. Make long-term plans for get togethers and reunions. Use having friends all over the world as an excuse to travel to far away places you might not have gone.

Just do it

Travel to see friends who have moved on is expensive. Traveling back to the place you left friends behind is expensive. Do it anyway.

Make Time

Sometimes friends travel back to the scene of the friendship crime. The timing almost always sucks. It may be a busy time of year. Maybe you've had a string of guests and all you've been doing is washing bed sheets. Make the effort and put aside the time anyway. If someone comes into town and invites you to lunch or coffee or dinner? Go. In the large scheme of your life it's an afternoon. Someday you might be the one traveling backwards, hoping your friends will put aside the time for a cup of coffee for you. Karma is a mocha flavored latte, my friends.

It's ok to make new friends

Not everyone you meet on your journey is going to be your BFF. Not everyone you meet is going to bring you to tears when it comes time to say goodbye. And that's ok. You're moving on, they're moving on. You have to live your life, and so do they. They will make new friends, and so will you, it's the nature of the beast. You can honor the time you spent together and put it in a little special box somewhere. The hard truth is there are people who you meet, maybe even people who you really, really like, who you will likely never see again. It's ok to be sad about it. None of that takes away from what you shared.

Just because there are new friends filling in the blank spaces doesn't negate or diminish the friendship *you* shared. It's like having another kid. You don't love the first one any less–your heart expands to love the next one just as much.

Losing friends is never easy, no matter how many times you do it. Keeping those friends, especially when they're hopping around the globe, is hard too.

But hard is different from impossible.

So as you get ready to say goodbye to good friends or casual acquaintances, or your BFF, whether you're the one staying or going, remember, don't cry because it's over. Smile because it happened.

And then go set up that messenger group.

QUESTIONS THAT KEEP YOU AWAKE AT NIGHT

What the hell have we done?

The big Kahuna question may haunt you for a while. The inquiry which fuels your nightmares... and your anxieties. While visions of burgers and Target dance in your head, you fret you've made the biggest mistake of your life. What were you thinking? What made you think you could pack up a house and the kids and a dog and move across the ocean? Were you smoking crack when your spouse brought it up? Under the influence of a cult leader? Drunk on the Kool-aid?

What on Earth were you thinking??

BOTH SIDES NOW
2017

"I hope that as she crossed that finish line, the promise of both sides beckoned."

Yesterday, as competitors in the Ironman Challenge raced past our apartment, pushing their bodies to the limit of endurance, I was slowly cycling toward an afternoon meant to celebrate the life of a woman who endured in a different way, who pushed her body to a different limit.

I knew *about* her long before we met. When she first got sick, she was the center of a buzz of activity: meals were cooked and delivered, the dog walked, company provided, magazines collected. I've seen this hive at work before, women swooping in and taking a slice of another woman's burden as her own. It amazes me every time, and makes me grateful to be a part of this womanhood.

Over time, as her illness ebbed and flowed I met her in person, but it was through my writing she got to know me, and I her. Somehow these words and sentences reached out and connected us in the way that stories have been connecting humans since the beginning of time. Our shared experiences became the thread that tied us together. The knots were newer and looser than the ones which connected her to others, but no matter. Once tied, you're forever knotted into the fabric of a life, no matter how loosely.

Recently her body reached its limit. All those binds and ties and knots were teased apart and released, but not before they came together one final time to weave a rich and colorful tapestry. Yesterday was meant to be a celebration of that tapestry–of that life–and I was honored to be included.

Yet as her husband talked to us about her wishes after death, I felt sightly fraudulent. Surely all of those people knew her so much better than I had, surely they were more deserving of this celebration.

He continued, shifting between Danish and English, and I caught the song playing in the background.

I've looked at clouds from both sides now,
from up and down, and still somehow
it's cloud illusions I recall.
I really don't know clouds at all.

It's impossible for me to associate Joni Mitchell's *Both Sides Now* with anything other than the moment Emma Thompson faces the truth of her husband's infidelity in *Love, Actually*. It's one of those snapshots of everyday life which make you question if love—and fear and happiness and anger—all the emotions that boil and bubble together to make a life, are worth the pain of loss. The soundtrack to that scene is part funeral dirge, part broken heart. It is mournful, haunting, and rueful, the warble of a woman who has seen, lived, loved. And lost.

We're allowed merely a glimpse of pain before the character swipes at her eyes, straightens the bed sheet, and throws open the door with a forced smile. Endurance of a completely different kind than those athletes hurtling toward a finish line.

Those sixty or so seconds of music and emotion get me every, single time. Yesterday was no exception.

Yet the day was not about mourning a death, but celebrating a life. There was food and wine, music, bright colors and funny quotes. No one seemed to be weighed down by the mantle of her death, what there was instead, present in every breath, was life. Hers, and ours, and in that moment, the culmination of the two.

Both sides now. Life and death, before and after, with and without.

At the end of the afternoon I cycled back home. The athletes were still going, doggedly pedaling by, pushing their bodies to the max. Most of them had a literal marathon still in front of them. It is a stamina I don't possess, but then perhaps, none of us realize the strength we have until we are tested. Endurance, after all, comes in many forms.

To swipe at your eyes, straighten your bed sheets, and throw open the door to the unknown.

Is it worth it? How can it not be? I hope that when she threw open that last door it was not with a forced smile, but with the knowledge that her life, though ended, will still live on in the knots of ours, in the stories we tell to connect to one another.

I hope that as she crossed that finish line, the promise of both sides beckoned.

Fly free, Trish. May you look at clouds from both sides now.

CALENDAR GIRL (noun):

The expert expat who is able to plan a year's worth of holidays 18 months in advance.

As in: *Easy Jet is having a sale for summer next year, let's book now!*

Wine and Cheese (Definitions)

LESSONS FROM A BROAD ABROAD
2014

"They are lessons you can pack up and take with you wherever you may be."

In a few short weeks, several good friends will pack up their homes and board flights bound for somewhere new. Some have known the stack of their deck for a while. Some knew the hand they were holding before they touched down in Copenhagen, knew their time here had a sell-by date. Others have been blindsided or taken by surprise. Job restructuring, illness, a change of circumstance.

Yet whether they've been here for one year or seven, whether their Denmark whistle-stop was a one-time only thing or simply another station on their express, there is little doubt their time abroad has changed them.

These are the ups and downs of an expatriate life.

Sometimes, the very fact of living in another country can be the single most important factor influencing your day-to-day life. My first year in Cyprus was tough. Given the opportunity to go home in those first few weeks, I would have been packed and on the first west-bound plane out of Laranca airport before you could say *yasas*. The initial adjustment to life away can be brutal, and often you are doing it alone.

Amazingly, the vast majority of us stick it out, which is lesson number one: **you are stronger than you think**. I stuck it out, sometimes for no other reason than sheer pig-headedness. Nearly six years later, I'm grateful I did. I'm grateful for many reasons, but I'm heartily grateful for the lessons being out of my home country and out of my comfort zone have taught me.

I've learned how to look at my home country from a different perspective.

It's easier to view the whole, to see the good and the bad, to see what works and what doesn't, when you're standing on the outside looking in. It's a unique perspective, and a powerful one. That first year I was the proverbial kid in the candy store, nose pressed up against the glass, mouth watering, salivating over everything I couldn't have, everything I missed. Six years on, I'm more of a discerning window shopper. I appreciate the fine chocolate but I'm better at spotting the stuff that's going to rot your teeth and make you sick.

I've learned to look for the common denominator.

I don't go to church. Or vote Republican. I still eat gluten, I don't do yoga, I drink wine. I don't have girls, I don't work outside the home, I have tattoos and I'm American. Any of those things could be seen as deal breakers in the friendship game. But I **am** an expat. I'm an expat living in a particular situation that many others are experiencing on the same plane of time and space. If you're smart, you realize sometimes that **one** common denominator is all you need.

I've learned absence does make the heart grow fonder.

Instead of feeling obligated to spend six hours in Thanksgiving traffic, seeing my family for only a handful of dates each year means I better appreciate the time I spend with them. Yes, it's hard sometimes, on my side as well as theirs, but I've learned that quality counts for a lot.

I've learned to trust my spouse.

It's no easy thing to place your trust in a job that requires you to give up everything you've known, pack it into boxes and move 7,000 miles away. I've had to remind myself at times that my husband does not take that trust lightly, and that every decision we've made is one that benefits not only his career, but us as a family. Twice in my life I've stepped off a plane in a country I'd never been to and led to a home I'd never seen. A home which my husband picked out after ticking off a list of impossible expectations and requirements that I've given him. Trust.

I've learned I can do things I didn't think I could do.
Drive on the other side of the road, commute by bicycle. I've learned how adjust and even thrive in another country. In many ways, I've adapted to this life better than my husband. Though the changes were greater for me, the benefits have been greater at times too.

I've learned I am not defined by any one thing.
Going from a part-time working mother in New York City to a suburban housewife in Nicosia was an adjustment for me. I lost my way for a while, trying to recreate my persona. But I have learned I can redefine myself as necessary--without losing any part of the whole.

I've learned there's life beyond New York.
I still think it's the best city in the world. I still think my two decades there molded me into the person I am. I still miss the restaurants and the shopping and the energy. But I can recall Central Park in fall with fondness, and also an understanding that after six years out of NYC, there may not be a place for me. And (deep breath) that's ok.

I've learned home is where you are all together, but also that there's nothing quite like going home, which makes it that much more special.

I've learned Goya Black Beans really are the best canned black beans and anything else is merely an inferior substitute.
Things are things. I can't find good black beans, but I can find great licorice and tea and fresh vegetables. Life as an expat is like sitting astride a giant scale. There are advantages, disadvantages, good and bad. If you get it right, the scales will balance. Spend too much time lamenting the loss of things and it's going to dip and sway and make your stomach drop in ways that you won't like.

I've learned that given time, you can adjust to almost any situation, even if adjusting means moving on.

I've learned that raising kids to embody certain cultural expectations is really, really hard when you don't have an entire country backing you up.

I've learned that saying goodbye is never easy, but also that people come in and out of your life for reasons which you may not be aware of. Those who are meant to stay in your life will, as long as you make the effort to keep them there.

Most of all I've learned that these lessons, whether learned through laughter or tears, are lessons you carry with you for the rest of your life. They are lessons you can pack up and take with you wherever you may be; lessons which continue to enrich your life whether you're making another whistle-stop on your lifelong tour or if you're hopping down for good and heading home.

PRO TIP

Always say goodbye!

It's important to say goodbye, in whatever language you choose, in whatever language you're comfortable in, in whatever language you have come to love or hate. Maybe you *won't* see those people again, but that fact doesn't negate the time you had with them. Honor that. Say goodbye.

You..yes, YOU...you may not think you've made an impact, but you have, whether it was on a small level or a big one, for a long time or short. Whether you're coming or going or staying put.

So adieu, adieu to you and you and YOU.

DEAR OLD FRIENDS
2018

"I remember you all."

I hope by now you've settled wherever it is you've ended up. Maybe it is home. Or perhaps it's another new country, another funky currency. I hope your shipment made it through customs. I hope the packers were gentle. If you've already watched with surprise and delight as the big trailer pulled up, I hope your boxes are emptied, even the one you didn't manage to unpack from the last move. Or the move before that. I hope you've found all the hardware to go with the Ikea furniture the movers made you take apart before they would ship it.

I hope your landing, whichever continent, was soft.

It never actually *is*, but you know what I mean.

While you're busy, busy, busy getting settled, plastering a smile on your face and meeting new people, while you are remembering names and comforting anxious kids, I just want you to know I haven't forgotten you. While you're getting the lay of the land, sometimes just making it through the day, there are things going on back here, in the place you left, that remind me of you.

Maybe it's a conversation or a question, a song, or a tradition you used to be a part of. Maybe it's the way someone takes their coffee or a child who reminds me of one of yours, a joke or a comment I want to share.

You wouldn't believe what happened! I want to tell you.

But when I turn, you're no longer there.

I should reach out more. I should message or email. I should send a quick note when I run smack into a reminder of the time we spent together. But the days are busy and suddenly it's nighttime and then Christmas and all my British friends start to harass me about Brussels sprouts and good intentions get lost in the shuffle.

I haven't forgotten you.

Whenever I hear of Scouts I can't help but think of Amanda, and I can't see a pavlova without thinking of Taryn. I think of Jill and laugh when someone asks for mayonnaise and anytime someone tells me three kids are tough, I think of Marta and her five. When I see pink ribbons I think of Dani and Ainsely and now Sara and whenever I'm lucky enough to procure a can of Goya black beans I think of the steady stream of American families who have marched across my path like the ants go marching through that childhood song. A banana in a purse reminds me of Annabel and cans of Red Bull make me think of Erna's over-caffeinated night.

You're all there, in my memories.

Some of you have been gone so long I can't remember whose paths crossed whose. The time line gets confused. Others left so recently the imprint of your time here is still fresh, not yet swept away by the tides of change.

I remember you all.

You've all left your mark, in one way or another, in ways big and small. Katie's eternal cheerfulness and Jennifer's optimism, Maggie's deep and even calm, the way Claire forgave me for dropping a weight on her toe.

Just because you're gone doesn't mean I've forgotten about you.

I run across reminders, across memories. What do you think of this? I want to ask a different Claire. Have you seen this article, I want to ask Roop. A photo pops up on a Facebook feed and I see Jo. Olive trees remind me of Katy and the buzz of a vuvuzela will forever make me think of Liesl, whose moved three different times since I saw her last.

Where has the time gone? Sometimes the memories get blurry around the edges, colors bleeding like postcards left on the fridge in the sun. But the shapes are still there.

I see your shadows in the things I do.

Don't worry. You're still there. You're not forgotten.

In case I haven't told you lately, I miss you. The days are filled with the things days are filled with. But in those quiet moments where I have the breath to reflect on this crazy life, I miss you all and the you-shaped holes you left behind when you moved on.

I hope you've settled in, whether you've just moved on or you're getting ready to move again. I hope the movers didn't pack the butter, or that bowl you left out in the kitchen by mistake. I hope you can take your booze with you.

I hope you're making memories wherever you are.

In case I haven't told you, I haven't forgotten you.

Love,
Me

AFTERWORD

It was only supposed to be two years.

Yet here I am a decade later.

My Big Apple babies? They've lived in Copenhagen longer than anywhere else. They've lived outside the United States longer than inside those nifty fifty. Ten years! I still fret, sometimes daily. I worry about roots: uprooting, down-rooting, re-routing. I can't pin down their accents. Will they end up on the *tuh-may-toe* side of the fence or will they land squarely on the *toe-mah-toe* side?

I shake my son's Magic 8-ball and ask: *Where the hell are we all going to end up?*

The answer is usually *reply hazy, try again*.

The concerns don't go away the longer we're away. As my children get older, the questions get bolder. Not *will they be on track in math class*, but *where are they going to go to college*? Not *when will we go 'home'*, but **can** we? We're moving away from *where do we want the kids to finish school* to *where do we want to retire?*

Ten years is a long time. What feels natural now is not the same as what felt natural when we started this journey a decade ago. The language I use is different. My friendships too. My taste, what I eat, how I dress, how I get around town. How I think and what I think about.

When we packed up our Brooklyn apartment and boarded a plane ten years ago the world was a very different place. There's more upheaval now, more turmoil. There are more planes falling out of the sky and more school shootings in the country I was raised in. There are seismic cultural shifts.

Equally, there's been a seismic shift **within**.

I am different.

Living abroad, away from home, has fundamentally changed who I am. My experiences are no longer pushed through a sieve of Americanness, but through a sieve of 'other".

148

I still struggle to pin down the concept of home. Is it where you lay your head? Where you're all together? Where your memories are made? What happens when you live someplace—or some places—longer than you lived in the place which formed your identity? What happens when your *kids* do?

A decade on the answers are no clearer.

More than anything else this journey has been a giant experiment. On my better days I fancy myself an expat Margaret Mead, standing on the sidelines scribbling notes about this tribe of expatriates I live and love among.

Is it hard? Yes.

Is it great? Yes again.

Is it messy and lovely and confusing and frustrating? Check, check, check.

Would I change it all if I could?

Not in a million years.

ABOUT THE AUTHOR

After twenty years in the Big Apple, Dina Honour left New York City for what was *meant* to be a two year stint in Cyprus. Ten years and another country later, she has her head firmly stuck in the damp, Danish soil. Since 2012, she's been writing about her personal experiences as an expat, a parent raising third-culture children, and the challenges and joys of living abroad.

Her writing has been recognized for excellence both in and outside of the United States, where it has appeared both online and in print. You can follow her blog, Wine and Cheese (Doodles), her author site at Dina Honour, or find her on social media platforms like Instagram, Twitter, and FaceBook.

Most of the essays included here first appeared in some format on her blog, Wine and Cheese (Doodles). Some have been modified, others are included here for the first time.

Her first novel, *All the Spaces in Between* is represented by the Robert Ledecker Agency. She is currently finishing up work on a second, *Daughters of Pax*.

Dina currently lives in Scandinavia with her husband and two sons.

Made in United States
Orlando, FL
05 December 2021

11178325R00096